I Can't Believe It's
Food Storage

A SIMPLE STEP-BY-STEP PLAN FOR USING
FOOD STORAGE TO CREATE DELICIOUS MEALS

CRYSTAL GODFREY

*To my parents, Bill and Rosalie Farnbach, who taught
me how to cook; my husband, Matt, for taste-testing the
recipes; and Lorraine Ohrmund, for teaching me that
anything is possible—one can at a time.*

Please Review This Book on Amazon.com or Deseretbook.com

If you like this book enough to award it four or five stars on Amazon.com or Deseretbook.com, let us know and we'll send you a free recipe you can't find anywhere else!

Your review can be as short as two or three sentences, or as long as you like. Please explain what you liked about the book—and why. Once your review appears on Amazon.com or Deseretbook.com, email us at marketing@leatherwoodpress.com, and we'll send you a fantastic new recipe from Crystal.

Walnut Springs Press, LLC
110 South 800 West
Brigham City, Utah 84302
http://walnutspringspress.blogspot.com

ISBN: 978-1-93521-717-6

Table of Contents

INTRODUCTION

Introduction

You Mean I Can Actually *Eat* My Food Storage?

What if I told you that in a very short time, I can teach you how to make delicious, nutritious food for your family faster and cheaper using your food storage? You're probably thinking that the words *delicious* and *food storage* don't belong in the same sentence, and I don't blame you. I used to feel that way too. But I promise that you will be pleasantly surprised as you try my easy, step-by-step plan. Soon you will be using your food storage on a daily basis in your favorite recipes, and your family will say, "I can't believe it's food storage!"

This book is perfect for you if:

- You want to start or maintain your food storage.
- You want to use your food storage rather than just letting it sit on a shelf.
- You want to actually *enjoy* eating meals made with food storage.
- You want the peace of mind of knowing that you will have food for your family if something goes wrong—and that your family will actually eat the food.

Isn't Food Storage Only for Emergencies?

You're Already Using It!

Here's how a typical conversation about food storage might sound:

> Wife: "Uh, do we want [food storage item]?"
>
> Husband: "What do you do with that?"
>
> Wife: "I don't know, but it's on the list."
>
> Husband: (sighs) "Well, if everything has blown up around me and there were nothing else to eat . . . (long pause) I guess I could eat it."

Guess what? You're probably already eating food storage. Do you ever use a pancake or muffin mix that says, "Just add water"? Surprise! That mix contains food storage items. How about a brownie or cake mix that doesn't call for milk? Yep, you guessed it—food storage. Go ahead and take a moment to get over the shock. Those mixes usually contain powdered milk, powdered eggs, or both, depending on the mix. And since you and your family have been eating items made with these mixes, it turns out you DO like food storage!

It's Not Just for the End of the World

Food storage isn't just for natural disasters or other widespread emergencies when food is unavailable for purchase, although it will definitely come in handy then. Think about these scenarios: *You forgot that you were supposed to take something to the ward dinner that starts in an hour. You went to bed thinking that you had plenty of milk for the next morning, only to find that someone put the empty carton in the refrigerator. You can't finish preparing a meal because you're out of an important ingredient. It's 5:00 p.m., and you haven't thought about dinner yet.* Having a working food storage will help you survive not only a major emergency but all the everyday emergencies as well.

The full benefits of food storage aren't realized when it sits on the shelf until disaster strikes or when it is used only occasionally. When you use your food storage regularly, you can save money, eat healthier, never run out of anything, and prepare meals faster. Most importantly, using your food storage every day is invaluable preparation for a potentially life-threatening emergency.

How Is Your Food Storage?

How long could your family live as it normally does without going to a grocery store?

How long do you think your family could **survive** *without going to a store?*

How much nonperishable food (the type that doesn't need refrigeration) do you have on hand?

Through His prophets, the Lord has commanded His people to store food in preparation for times of need. President Ezra Taft Benson said, "The revelation to store food may be as essential to our temporal salvation today as boarding the ark was to the people in the days of Noah. . . . For the righteous, the gospel provides a warning before a calamity, a program for the crises, a refuge for each disaster. The Lord has . . . warned us of famines, but the righteous will have listened to prophets and stored at least a year's supply of survival food" (Ezra Taft Benson, *God, Family, Country: Our Three Great Loyalties* [Salt Lake City: Deseret Book, 1974], 267, 269).

If you haven't started your food storage or don't know how to use what you do have, you're not alone. Many of those who do have food storage don't reap the full benefits of a three-month supply and a one-year supply, which modern prophets counsel us to have. Generally speaking, this failure is not due to lack of faith or motivation, but to the fact that people don't know how to use food storage in their everyday recipes.

Making Food Storage Simple

The Philosophy behind This Book

If you've ever visited my website, www.everydayfoodstorage.net, you know that I have a simple, fun approach to helping people cook with food storage. You might also notice that teaching others what I've learned is my passion! My website contains tasty recipes, handouts to share, how-to videos, and comments from people like you. And because you see it and read about it on my website, you know that I personally use my food storage every day in delicious and easy-to-make meals that save me time and money.

I decided to write this book after seeing so many people fail when they tried to follow the prophets' counsel about food storage. Most people do too much at once and wind up miserable, with nothing to show for it that they can really eat. Each of us struggles. Some people are single with kids to feed, some are out of work trying to make ends meet, and others are struggling just to find time to make a healthy dinner for their family. Food storage can relieve all of these burdens when used every day—if you just know how to do it.

What's in It for You?

Chances are, you've already tried to build your food storage. Chances are, you've tried to get your family to eat some food storage item, or you've researched food storage and found some very unappetizing recipes. You may think food storage is complicated and burdensome, yet you want to follow the prophets' counsel.

I promise that you can have all the benefits and blessings that come with having a three-month supply of food and a one-year supply of food. You just need to learn the secret of how to do it so your family will eat it!

That is why I created a step-by-step food-storage training program that will teach you how to transition into using food storage every day in your own recipes—at a comfortable pace.

As you follow the principles in this book, you won't have to eat strange or tasteless food, and I won't confuse you or put you to sleep. The principles in this book are fun, simple, and doable. In just a few hours, you will learn everything you need to know to start collecting and eating your food storage TODAY!

My Story

I'll never forget when I had my "a-ha" moment about food storage. My husband and I were visiting my parents in Southern California. We desperately needed a vacation since we each worked three or four jobs to make ends meet. Nine months previously, we had moved to Utah for a new job. Life was great—we had just purchased our first home and were expecting our first baby. Everything was going so well and then it happened: my husband was unexpectedly laid off. We got all the extra jobs we could fit into our schedule and were working a combined 120 hours a week. I was pregnant, tired, and husband-deprived . . . hence, the very needed vacation.

It was Sunday and we were attending church when my friend got up to speak. She held up some yellow daffodils and explained that an enormous meadow in the San Bernardino Mountains is filled with the beautiful flowers. My friend explained that people come from all over the country to view the breathtaking site. In the middle of these daffodils is a modest A-frame home with a sign out front that says, "Answers to the Questions I Know You Are Asking: 50,000 bulbs, one at a time, by one woman, two hands, two feet, and one brain. Began in 1958."

This magnificent field of flowers didn't happen overnight, and it wasn't created by an army of gardeners. It was created one bulb at a time by one woman. Likewise, any of us can do almost anything, as long as we approach it one step at a time. As the Lord Himself declared, "And out of small things proceedeth that which is great" (D&C 64:33–34).

A Life Lesson—One Can at a Time

As you've probably guessed by now, my friend used the daffodil story to introduce the topic of food storage. She went on to explain that obtaining, storing, and using food storage isn't complicated. Just as the woman with the field of daffodils planted one bulb at a time, my friend said, we can build our food storage one can at a time. All we need is two hands, two feet, and one brain.

She made food storage sound so easy, but I wondered, *Can I really make it a part of my everyday life?* Like most people, I had always thought of food storage as emergency-only food, assuming it was difficult to cook with and would never taste good. In fact, I had secretly hoped I could get through life without having to learn how to use food storage! But with my husband's job situation fresh on my mind, I knew I had to, for my family's sake.

I had no idea that I would soon completely change my attitude about food storage, or that in just six months I would have my food storage and would use it every day.

Three-Month Supply and One-Year Supply

I began with the following counsel from a Church pamphlet: "Build a small supply of food that is part of your normal, daily diet. One way to do this is to purchase a few extra items each week to build a one-week supply of food. Then you can gradually increase your supply until it is sufficient for three months. . . . For longer-term needs, and where permitted, gradually build a supply of food that will last a lot longer and that you can use to stay alive, such as wheat, white rice and beans." (*All is Safely Gathered In*, Feb. 2007). While the three-month supply made sense to me, I wasn't yet sold on the one-year supply. I couldn't think of a single recipe that combined dried beans, powdered milk, whole-wheat kernels, sugar, and salt to make anything that my family would eat.

However, I did find a "Random Sampler" article in the *Ensign* that gave great advice about wheat—advice that seemed applicable to all long-term food-storage items: "Use wheat in recipes your family already likes. Then it is not totally unfamiliar and you know the recipe is good. Try wheat in desserts first—who can turn down a cookie? Do not feel you must use 100% whole wheat. Half white (all-purpose) flour and half whole-wheat flour gives excellent results" (Rosalie Farnbach, "Whole Wheat—in Disguise," *Ensign*, Aug. 1990, 71).

As I'm sure you do, I realized that I already used many recipes that called for milk, sugar, flour (which is just ground-up wheat), beans, salt, etc. Since food storage is a basic set of storable food items that can be used in a wide range of recipes, I decided, why not my own recipes—every day?

So I tried some food storage in my next batch of cookies. Guess what? They tasted great, and my family didn't even notice the difference. I practiced cooking with whole wheat, then powdered milk, and so on until it became second nature for me to cook with a wide variety of long-term food-storage items. I discovered that long-term food storage coupled with a three-month supply can make a wide range of delicious foods.

But What If My Food Storage Floats Down the River?

I still had one major fear—a fear that affects many people when they think about food storage: *What if my food storage gets damaged, destroyed, or stolen when I need it most?* But I took courage from the words of Elder Vaughn J. Featherstone, "Now what about those who would plunder and break in and take that which we have stored for our families' needs? Don't give this one more idle thought. There is a God in heaven whom we have obeyed. Do you suppose he would abandon those who have kept his commandments? He said, 'If ye are prepared, ye shall not fear'" (Vaughn J. Featherstone, "Food Storage," *Ensign*, May 1976, 116).

The Lord won't abandon us. In fact, He has declared that if we obey Him, He is bound to bless us (see D&C 82:10). In my opinion, this divine declaration applies to the commandment to obtain our food storage just as it applies to any other commandment.

Assistance from a Higher Source

Now I can see that I didn't actually accomplish anything on my own. The sacrament-meeting talk about food storage came at the perfect time. I found the food and other items on sale just when I needed them. Miracles happened all around, and we found ways to save money so we didn't go into debt. Most importantly, I was inspired how to use my food storage in recipes—and how to use it every day. The Lord wanted my family to have and use food storage, and He wants the same for you.

As Nephi said, "I know that the Lord giveth no commandments unto the children of men, save he shall prepare a way for them that they may accomplish the thing which he commandeth them" (1 Ne. 3:7). Relatedly, President Kimball remarked, "The Lord will not translate one's good hopes and desires and intentions into works. Each of us must do that for himself" (Spencer W. Kimball, *The Miracle of Forgiveness* [Salt Lake City: Bookcraft, 1969], 8).

Now It's Your Turn

The Lord has prepared a way for you to obey His commandment to obtain and use long-term food storage. Once you start down that path, you will start to receive the blessings He has in store for you and your family. As Elder Featherstone proclaimed, "The Lord will make it possible, if we make a firm commitment, for every Latter-day Saint family to have a year supply of food reserves . . . All we have to do is to decide, commit to do it, and then keep the commitment. Miracles will take place; the way will be opened" ("Food Storage," 116).

You can have the blessings of being prepared. You can have your food storage, and you can actually eat it and enjoy it! You can do it easily and on your own schedule, and you can target it to your family's specific needs. It's just that simple.

The Program

Making It Easy for You

Now, you're ready for action. And since you're busy fixing meals, spending time with your family, and now, starting your food storage, I've made it easy for you to multitask. I've designed three family home evening lessons to get your family involved and help you plan your three-month supply. Together, you will set a time for family dinner, learn about balanced meals, pick meals you all like to eat, find and organize recipes into a menu or food-themed days, and then inventory your specific needs for a three-month supply.

Next, you'll learn basic cooking concepts for each of the long-term food-storage items: powdered milk, powdered eggs, whole wheat, dried beans, and dried fruits and vegetables. Think of me as your personal food storage trainer! I'm going to teach you one concept and its benefits, help you see the concept in action, then encourage you to use the concept in my recipes and/or your own recipes before moving to the next concept. Within the training program, you will also find shopping tips, ideas for finicky eaters, hints for dealing with everyday emergencies, and basic guidelines for storing food for long periods of time.

You'll be surprised at how easy it is to make delicious meals with your food storage—and at how prepared you'll feel!

The Secret

Before we begin, it is imperative that you understand the biggest must-do of this program: *You must promise not to tell your family!* Your family will eat what you are making with food storage items, *if you don't warn them first.* If you tell people that something is made with food storage before they try it, they might refuse to try it. And trust me—there is nothing better than sitting back and watching someone rant and rave about how he doesn't like whole wheat while he's wolfing down a 100% whole-wheat cookie.

Remember, you can have your food storage and eat it, too!

STEP 1
GETTING YOUR FAMILY INVOLVED

STEP 1

GETTING YOUR FAMILY INVOLVED

Planning Your Three-Month Supply

In Step 2, you'll actually build your three-month supply of food. But in order to decide what to store, you'll need your family's input. After all, can you remember each food item that your family enjoys that could be stored for three months? And can you remember every ingredient in their favorite meals? To enlist your family's help, I've developed three family home evening lessons. These lessons combine gospel principles with practical life skills such as participating in family dinnertime, understanding recipes, and preparing balanced meals. Following each lesson are action steps for you to take before the next lesson. Once you've finished the three lessons, you'll be able to easily create a three-month supply inventory that is specific to your family.

Family Home Evening Lesson #1
"Come and Dine"

This lesson focuses on the importance of eating together as a family. There is no better place than the dinner table for family members to discuss their day, create memories. and to enjoy an atmosphere of love and laughter. Eating dinner together as a family helps your children know that they are your priority.

According to the U.S. Department of Health and Human Services, family mealtimes are important because:

(1) When you regularly eat with your children, your meals are more likely to be healthy and balanced. (2) Compared to teens that have frequent family dinners, those who rarely have family dinners are three and a half times more likely to abuse prescription drugs or an illegal drug other than marijuana. (3) Girls who have five or more meals a week with their families are one-third less likely to develop unhealthy eating habits, which can range from skipping meals to abuse of diet pills to full-fledged anorexia. (4) Parental influence and involvement is an important tool in preventing substance abuse. Regularly sitting down for a meal with your children is one way to connect with them and be involved with what is happening in their lives. ("Get Involved: the Importance of Family Mealtime,": http://family.samhsa.gov/get/mealtime.aspx)

It is critical to have dinner at a set time every day so that each family member can plan to be there. A great way to get everyone excited about dinner is to have each family member help plan and prepare the meal. In this family home evening lesson, you'll teach the importance of family meals, decide on a set time for dinner, and make a list of everyone's favorite meals.

Action Steps

Prepare a list of meals you could make in little time and with little mess in case of an everyday emergency. Your family will choose their favorites from this list. Also, prepare a list of the meals you make most often, just in case your family needs a few to get them started on their list of favorites.

Preparation

- Have a sheet of paper and pen or pencil for each family member.
- Have a set of scriptures handy.
- Create sentence starter slips (see "Game: When I was Five or Six or Something," pg. 24), then fold them and place them in a hat prior to FHE.
- Write a list of everyday emergency meals your family enjoys (for example, freezer lasagna, chicken noodle soup, and chili).

Purpose

1. Share the meaning behind and importance of eating together as a family.
2. Schedule a consistent time and place for family dinner.
3. Involve the family in planning and preparing for family meals.

Thought

"Perhaps nothing is as unifying in the course of a family's week as to eat together" (Jeffrey R. Holland, Roundtable Discussion, Worldwide Leadership Training Meeting, Feb. 9, 2008).

Song

"A Song of Thanks," *Children's Songbook*, no. 20

Scripture

"Behold, I stand at the door, and knock: if any man hear my voice, and open the door, I will come in to him, and will sup with him, and he with me" (Revelations 3:20).

Story

Tell the story of Jesus feeding His disciples at the sea of Tiberias, as found in John 21:1–17.

Explanation

Jesus had a very important lesson to teach His disciples, and He chose to do it during a meal. Julie B. Beck, General Relief Society President, stated,

> He [Jesus] had a fire there and coals and fish, and He said, "Come and dine." Now, that describes quite a bit of preparation. A meal had been prepared—a family meal, you could say—and He invited them to come and dine, not just run in and eat, but come and dine. And then the scripture says, "When they had dined." He then began to teach them that wonderful teaching about feeding His sheep (see John 21:9–15). There is something about eating together and mellowing out and having that feeling there . . . He created the setting for that marvelous teaching, and it was a mealtime. And I think that wasn't

accidental. (Julie B. Beck, Roundtable Discussion, Worldwide Leadership Training Meeting, Feb. 9, 2008)

Family Discussion

1. Discuss why it is important for your family to set a specific dinnertime. Then decide on a time that works best for everyone. Be sure to plan enough time for everyone to help prepare the meal, eat the meal, and help clean up.

2. Get everyone involved, and let each family member have a say in what the family eats. Give each person a piece of paper and ask him or her to write down his or her ten favorite homemade meals. If you have young children, you may want to write down what they say. (If you're worried about only hearing "macaroni and cheese" or "chicken nuggets," give options of meals and have children choose their favorites.)

3. Get out your list of everyday-emergency meals and have your family vote as to which ones they like best. Write down the meals in order of popularity.

Game: When I Was Five or Six or Something

Have family members share their most memorable dinnertime stories by drawing one of the following sentence starters out of a hat and finishing it with a dinnertime memory. You can ask only the person who pulled out the starter to answer it, or have everyone answer.

When I was five or six or something, I remember dinner being . . .

My earliest dinner table memory is . . .

My favorite part about eating together as a family is . . .

The funniest time at the dinner table was when . . .

My favorite meal my mom makes is . . .

If I could have a perfect meal, it would be . . .

Family Home Evening Lesson #2
"The Recipe for Eternal Life"

Introduction

In this lesson, you will teach your family the importance of recipes, how to read a recipe, and how to find recipes in a cookbook. You will also teach the Lord's recipe for eternal life as taught by Elder L. Tom Perry during April 2008 General Conference. Helping your family become familiar with a recipe will get them in the kitchen with you. When children are busy measuring, pouring, and spreading, they don't realize that they are learning.

Getting your children to help you in the kitchen can be a great learning experience. According to the Penn State Cooperative Extension:

- "Cooking involves reading and talking. There is much to talk about as a recipe is read, followed, and prepared.

- Children learn math skills through counting, measuring, and following step-by-step directions.

- Science is learned as children see how food changes during cooking. They learn about hot and cold, floating and sinking, and dissolving, melting, and freezing.

- Good nutrition is encouraged through cooking. Seeing exactly what goes into a recipe helps children learn to make better decisions about the food they eat.

- Children can learn about and connect with other cultures as they prepare foods from various cultural groups.

- Thinking skills are developed as children learn to compare and make relationships in food preparation. If we use too much flour in our cookie recipe, the result is a dry, hard cookie. Proportions are easily mastered when children learn that if you double the ingredients in the cookie recipe, you get double the number of cookies.

Social skills are practiced in cooking when children work together, take turns, and solve problems. Most importantly, self-esteem abounds when children prepare foods for themselves and others."

("Kids Can Cook—and Learning Is the Secret Ingredient!" Penn State Cooperative Extension, http://betterkidcare.psu.edu/CaringForKids/CaringForKids3-5.pdf)

As you can see, there are numerous benefits to letting your family help you in the kitchen. In this lesson, your family will also help you locate the recipes for their favorite meals so that you can easily organize them into a binder. You'll love having all your recipes together in one place and organized into categories—you'll never have to search for a recipe again!

Action Steps

1. Decide If You Are a Menu Person or a Themed-Day Person

Now that you have a set time for dinner and have identified your family's favorite meals, it's time to create a plan that will allow you to cook the meals with little effort—and to make it a habit. Ask yourself: Am I a menu person? Menus help you plan and prepare in advance what you will eat, ensuring a variety of meals and making shopping simple. (Half of the battle of making dinner is deciding what to make, so it's great when you can simply look at your menu and have it already decided for you.) Plus, you can re-use a monthly menu and your family will never know.

On the other hand, you may have tried menus in the past and found that they don't work for you. If you're like me, you might prefer "themed days" to menus. With themed days, you organize your recipes into days—i.e., chicken day, casserole day, Italian night—allowing you to have part of the decision made while keeping some flexibility. As you plan your menus or themed days, try to do the following:

- Make sure you don't make the same meal more than twice a month. This will allow you to use a menu over and over yet still serve a wide variety of meals.

- Vary the types of meals throughout the week. Mix it up, making sure you have different meats (i.e. chicken, fish, beef, pork) and different types of meals (casseroles, roasts, salads, sandwiches, stir-fry, etc.) in the course of a week.

- Take into account your busiest days, and plan easier meals for those days. Look for meals or dishes you can make easily from leftovers. (Make sure you wait a few days so your family doesn't feel like they're eating the same thing again.)

2. Categorize Your Family's Favorite Meals

Categorize each of your family's favorite meals as either a summer meal or a winter meal. (You'll have a menu or themed days for both seasons.) Winter recipes are usually heartier, cooked in the oven, and served hot. Examples of winter meals are roasts, meat loaf, chili, and casseroles. Summer meals are grilled, microwaved, or cooked on the stovetop, and they are usually lighter. Summer meals might include hot dogs, stir-fry, burritos, sandwiches, or salads. Your family may have a favorite meal (such as pizza) that you cook year round, and it's okay if a few meals cross over from winter to summer.

Once you've grouped the meals into summer or winter meals, group the meals into seven categories. For example, my winter meal categories are roasts/company meals, casseroles, chicken, Italian, beef, Mexican, and soups. Categorizing your meals will ensure that you have a variety of foods on your menu—or make it easy to have themed days.

3. Round up Your Cookbooks

Get all your cookbooks together so that your family can help you find the recipes for their favorite meals.

Materials

- Print out and read Elder L. Tom Perry's April 2008 General Conference address titled "The Gospel of Jesus Christ" (see *Ensign*, May 2008).
- Have a set of scriptures handy.
- Print out the list of meals your family enjoys (from last week's lesson).
- Set out all the cookbooks that contain the recipes for the meals mentioned in last week's family home evening.

Purpose

1. Teach family members how to read and follow a basic recipe.
2. Discuss the Lord's recipe for eternal life as taught by L. Tom Perry.
3. Have family members help locate recipes for their favorite meals mentioned in last week's family home evening.

Thought

"Essentially, the gospel of Jesus Christ is a five-ingredient recipe for eternal life" (L. Tom Perry, "The Gospel of Jesus Christ," *Ensign*, May 2008, 44-46).

Song

"I Want to Live the Gospel," *Children's Songbook*, no. 148

Scripture

"For behold, this is my work and my glory—to bring to pass the immortality and eternal life of man" (Moses 1:39).

Object Lesson

Show your family a cookbook. Explain that cookbooks are books that contain recipes for different dishes. A recipe gives instructions on how to make a dish—a certain kind of food. If the directions are not followed correctly or if an ingredient is left out, the food might not taste good.

Briefly go over a recipe and explain how you would follow it.

Explanation

Ask your family members to close their eyes and think of eternal life, then describe the picture that comes to mind. Explain that eternal life and immortality are two different things. "Immortality is to live forever as a resurrected being. Through the Atonement of Jesus Christ, everyone will receive this gift. Eternal life, or exaltation, is to live in God's presence and to continue as families (see D&C 131:1–4). Like immortality, this gift is made possible through the Atonement of Jesus Christ" ("Eternal Life," *Gospel Topic Library*, www.lds.org).

Having a clear picture of eternal life helps us behave differently. When we have a clear picture of eternal life, we want to pray, read our scriptures, keep the law of chastity, be kind to everyone, and prepare to attend the temple. These things will prepare us to live together forever with our earthly family and with our Heavenly Father and our Savior Jesus Christ.

Family Discussion

Discuss how your family can follow the Lord's recipe for eternal life by going over the instructions as outlined by Elder L. Tom Perry.

The Lord's recipe for eternal life:

1. **Faith in Jesus Christ and His Atonement.** Discuss how family members can increase their faith in Jesus Christ and His Atonement. Elder Perry stated, "Faith in Jesus Christ and His Atonement turns us to Him. The world teaches that seeing is believing, but our faith in our Lord leads us to believe so we can see Him and the Father's plan for us. Our faith also leads to action—it leads to the commitments and changes associated with true repentance." (Perry, "The Gospel of Jesus Christ").

2. Repentance. Explain that repentance is key to preparing for baptism and to having the Holy Ghost as a constant companion to help us make correct choices. Elder Perry said, "The gift of the Holy Ghost is available only to those who are cleansed by repentance of the sins of the world" (Ibid).

3. Baptism by Immersion and the Gift of the Holy Ghost. "Those who are baptized enter into a covenant with God to take upon themselves the name of Jesus Christ, keep His commandments, and serve Him to the end (see Mosiah 18:8–10; D&C 20:37). Church members renew this covenant each time they partake of the sacrament (see D&C 20:77, 79).

   Those who keep the covenants they made at baptism are blessed by the Lord for their faithfulness. Some of the blessings include the constant companionship of the Holy Ghost, the remission of sins, and the privilege of being spiritually reborn. If they continue faithfully, they are promised eternal life (see 2 Nephi 31:19–20)" "Baptism," Gospel Topic Library, www.lds.org, http://lds.org/ldsorg/v/index.jsp?vgnextoid=bbd508f54922d010VgnVCM1000004d82620aRCRD&locale=0&index=2&sourceId=1af539b439c98010VgnVCM1000004d82620a____).

4. Enduring to the End. Explain that enduring to the end means being faithful until the end of our life. The Apostle Paul told Timothy, "I have fought a good fight, I have finished my course, I have kept the faith" (2 Timothy 4:7). Explain

that enduring isn't easy and that Heavenly Father intended for it to be difficult, challenging, and refining as we prepare to return to live with Him and receive eternal blessings.

Testimony

Share your testimony with your family about the importance of gaining eternal life. Stress your love for each family member as you explain why you want each member to be with you forever and why eternal life is the most important goal for your family.

Game: Recipe Scavenger Hunt

Take the list of recipes your family created last week and send family members on a scavenger hunt through your cookbooks to find the recipes. Make sure all your cookbooks are on your kitchen table or in another accessible location. When a family member finds a recipe, have him or her mark it with a sticky note for you to find later.

Family Home Evening Lesson #3
"The Word of Wisdom"

Your family now has a set time for dinner, and each member knows what a recipe is. In this lesson, your family will learn the last piece of the dinner puzzle: balancing a meal. Learning about healthy foods is a great time to talk about the guidelines the Lord has given us in the Word of Wisdom. Teaching your family healthy habits that will last a lifetime may help protect your loved ones from high cholesterol, high blood pressure, obesity, and adult-onset diabetes.

This lesson features a game called the Food Draft. In this game, your family helps you plan what to have for dinner and then practices putting together a healthy meal. Using this game is also a great way to prevent your family from complaining about dinner, since each family member now has ownership over what is served. You can plan the meals a week or a month at a time. Re-use the game and dinner cards at future family home evenings so that your family can regularly participate in planning and preparing meals. You can also take the game a step further and have the family member that chose the meal help you in the kitchen the day you plan on serving that meal. This gives you great one-on-one time with your family members, gets you some help in the kitchen, and teaches family members—all at the same time.

Action Steps

1. Place Copies of Your Family's Favorite Recipes in a Binder

This will be easy, since your family has already located their favorite recipes. Compiling your recipes will make it easier to inventory what you need to buy, and you won't have to spend a lot of time finding recipes or deciding what to serve for dinner. With the favorite recipes collected, you have three options: (1) make photocopies of the recipes, (2) type all the recipes on your computer, or (3) use a mix of copied and typed recipes. Making copies of all your recipes is the quickest way, but they won't look uniform when compiled. Typing your recipes will take more time and effort, but the style will be the same and you can easily print another page if needed.

2. Organize Your Recipe Binder

Make a title page for each recipe category, with a list of the different meal options. Use the title page as a divider, placing the corresponding recipes after the divider page in the same order listed on the page. Separate your winter and summer recipes with a page divider. Later, if you add a new recipe, just add it to the correct section, write it in at the bottom of your title page list, and keep going. Also, put the recipes in page protectors so that if you spill on your book, you can just wipe the pages off with a damp cloth.

3. Get Your Calendar Ready and Make Meal Cards for the Food Draft

In this family home evening lesson, your family will help you put together balanced meals for your menu (or for your food-themed days) using the Food Draft game. In this game, family members decide when they get to eat certain meals—and which side dishes go with which entrées. You can use this game to plan for a month or week at a time, whichever fits your family best.

- Make meal cards by writing the meal names on squares that will fit your calendar. If you're doing themed days, color coordinate the meal cards with your themed days of the week so that your family will know that certain meals belong on certain days.

- Create side-dish strips that can be glued to your meal cards to make a complete meal. Side dishes from which the family can choose may be green salad, potatoes, corn, peas, broccoli, squash, etc. Make two to three different side-dish strips for each available day. Because your family will choose side dishes from these strips, it's a great way to introduce some new vegetables. This will not only teach your family about balanced meals but ensure that they eat a variety of vegetables. It should also alleviate any battles over vegetables because, after all, your family—not you—chose the side dishes!

Preparation

- Read the Word of Wisdom (D&C 89) and the story of Daniel refusing to eat forbidden food and drink see (Daniel 1:1–20).

- Bring a set of scriptures.

- Visit http://www.mypyramid.gov/kids/index.html and print the "Tips for Families" handout, a 2-sided My Pyramid for Kids mini-poster with the "My Pyramid for Kids" graphic on one side, and eating and physical activity tips on the other.

- Have a calendar, meal cards, and side-dish strips available, along with a glue stick.

- Write each family member's name on a separate strip of paper and place strips in a hat or basket.

Purpose

1. Teach the importance of taking care of our bodies, minds, and spirits by obeying the Word of Wisdom.

2. Share the kinds of foods we should be eating as shown on the food pyramid.

3. Have family members practice pairing meals with side dishes to create well-balanced meals.

Thought

"May we continue to stand for physical, mental, and spiritual health through observance of the Word of Wisdom and receive the blessings predicated upon obedience to the word of the Lord," (N. Eldon Tanner, First Presidency Message: "Trusting the Lord's Promise," *Ensign*, Aug. 1981, 2).

Song

"The Word of Wisdom," *Children's Songbook*, no. 154

Scripture

"Yea, all things which come of the earth, in the season thereof, are made for the benefit and the use of man, both to please the eye and to gladden the heart: Yeah, for food and for raiment, for taste and for smell, to strengthen the body and to enliven the soul" (D&C 59:18–19).

Story

Tell the story of Daniel and his friends refusing to eat the king's meat and drink the king's wine (see Daniel 1:1–20).

Explanation

The Lord told Daniel how to keep his mind and body healthy and strong. Similarly, in 1833, the Lord told Joseph Smith how we can keep our minds alert and our bodies healthy. The revelation the Prophet Joseph received is called the Word of Wisdom. If we obey this law of good health, we will recieve wonderful blessings.

With your family, read D&C 89 and discuss how you can "find wisdom and great treasures of knowledge, even hidden treasures," and how you can "run and not be weary, and [can] walk and not faint" (D&C 89:19–20).

Family Discussion

Show your family the food pyramid chart and explain that a balanced meal contains grains, a variety of fruits and vegetables, and protein such as milk, meat, and beans. Discuss the tips for eating correctly and exercising to keep our bodies healthy.

Game: The Food Draft

This game gives family members the opportunity to choose when a main dish will be eaten and the side dishes to go along with it.

The Food Draft works similar to a sports draft. Once a person has chosen a main dish and side dishes, those items are no longer available for another night's meal. To begin, create an order for the draft by drawing family members' names out of the hat. Lay the main-dish cards, side-dish strips, and calendar on a board or table. Allow each family member to choose the main-dish card, side-dish strips, and day that meal will be eaten. Place the card and strips on the calendar.

Action Step

Inventory Your Recipes So You Know What to Buy

Congratulations! You've now had family home evening three weeks in a row, have taught your family valuable life skills, and are on your way to using food storage every day. It's now time to start compiling your three-month supply. Focus on stocking the ingredients you use most often in your family's favorite recipes. The best way to do this is to take inventory of the products you use regularly, and decide how much you would need to last for three months.

With all your family's favorite recipes in one binder, you can use your computer to quickly inventory the ingredients. For a FREE three-month supply inventory, visit my good friends at http://foodstoragemadeeasy.net/babysteps/step-3-three-months-of-normal-food/. Click on the "Training: Baby Steps" tab and under step #3, you'll find a great Microsoft Excel spreadsheet for inventorying what foods you'll need. (You don't need to be an Excel genius; the site has a very detailed how-to video.)

The Good Stuff

You're getting closer to having your three-month supply. Aren't you excited? With your family on board and your preparation for your supply complete, let's move on and get it done.

STEP 2

CREATING YOUR THREE-MONTH SUPPLY

STEP 2

CREATING YOUR THREE-MONTH SUPPLY

Why Do I Need a Three-Month Supply?

As we discussed in Step 1, a three-month food supply consists of foods that you and your family normally eat. If you rotate and use it, your three-month supply can be:

- An emergency fund you can eat
- A great way to never run out of anything again
- A guaranteed variety of cooking options

An Emergency Fund You Can Eat

According to Church leaders, in addition to setting aside money for emergencies, each family should have a three-month supply of food. President J. Reuben Clark stated, "When we really get into hard times, where food is scarce or there is none at all, and so with clothing and shelter, money may be no good for there may be nothing to buy, and you cannot eat money, you cannot get enough of it together to burn to keep warm, and you cannot wear it" (*Church News*, Nov. 21, 1953, 4). It's true! You can't eat money, but you can eat your three-month supply of food—if you have it and know how to use it.

Did you know that stored food provides a much higher return on investment than a savings account. Currently, the average interest rate for a savings account is just 0.41%. With food prices rising an average of 5.2% in 2008 and continuing to rise in 2009, you can clearly get a better return by storing food (see "Statement Savings National Average," http://bankrate.com/brm/publ/passbk.asp; and "Consumer Price Index Summary," http://www.bls.gov/news.release/cpi.nr0.htm; accessed March 2009). Therefore, having a supply of food is a good investment, especially during a time of inflation. Now you can rewind the clock on rising food prices, because the price of a can of wheat can't change when it's already in your cupboard. This gives your income time to adjust to the rising cost of living.

A Great Way to Never Run Out of Anything Again

Don't you hate it when you're cooking a dish and discover that you don't have one of the ingredients? It can ruin your day, not to mention your meal! With a three-month supply of food, you never run out of ingredients you regularly use, because you always have extras on hand. Now you can wait to purchase items until they are on sale or until you have a coupon, and the savings will allow you to buy even more extras. You will be able to make any favorite recipe at any time, with no more emergency trips to the store (no more wasted fuel!) and no more overspending for items at regular price.

It doesn't end there. Don't you hate running out of non-food items like soap, detergent, toothpaste, deodorant, and toilet paper? No doubt you can relate to folding paper towels into napkins for dinner, or trying to squeeze out enough toothpaste to get you through until morning! Now you can stop doing that, because you'll have a three-month supply of these household products.

A Guaranteed Variety of Cooking Options

A three-month supply of food gives you a myriad of options. Let's say you want to make a casserole that contains condensed cream soup, chicken, and vegetables. You can choose between chicken from your freezer and canned chicken, and you can use fresh, frozen, or canned vegetables. You can make your own cream soup or use the canned versions. With your three-month supply, you always have different options to choose from, depending on how much time you have.

When you don't have time to prepare dinner, wouldn't you like to have cheaper, faster options than the local pizza or burger joint? A three-month supply allows you the option of "everyday emergency" meals, such as freezer meals that you bake in the oven, boxed meals that take half an hour to prepare, or canned meals that can be ready in five minutes or less.

> *Tip: The next time you run out of something, buy two. It's a great way to start stocking up right now.*

Creating Your Three-Month Supply

First Things First: Food Your Family Eats

Want to start right now? Here is a handy food-storage pantry list. Per your family's input in Step 1, add or subtract items to suit their needs.

Suggested Foods for Three-Month Supply

Baking Items

Baking chips (milk chocolate, semisweet, white, butterscotch, etc.)

Baking chocolate squares (semisweet, unsweetened, white)

Baking cocoa

Baking powder

Baking soda

Biscuit/baking mix

Canned frosting

Coconut

Corn syrup

Cornstarch

Cream of tartar

Dried fruit (apricots, cranberries, raisins)

Extracts (almond, mint, vanilla)

Flour (all-purpose, bread, whole-wheat)

Food coloring

Gelatin

Honey

Instant pudding

Marshmallows

Milk (evaporated, sweetened condensed [or make your own from powdered milk])

Mixes (brownies, cake, cornbread, muffin, quick bread, etc.)

Nonstick cooking spray

Baking Items (continued)

Nuts (almonds, pecans, walnuts)
Oil (olive, vegetable)
Pie filling
Quick-cooking oats

Quick-cooking tapioca
Salt
Shortening
Sugar (brown, confectioners', granulated)

Canned Goods

Applesauce
Beans (black, great northern, kidney, etc.)
Broth (beef, chicken)
Condensed soup (chicken, mushroom, etc.)
Fruits (fruit cocktail, pineapple, etc.)
Green chiles
Ketchup
Mushrooms

Olives
Peanut butter
Salsa
Sauces (alfredo, spaghetti, taco, etc.)
Tomatoes (diced, paste, sauce, stewed, puréed)
Tuna
Vegetables (green beans, corn, etc.)

Seasonings

Bouillon granules (beef, chicken)
Garlic
Onion soup mix
Taco seasoning

Vinegar (cider, red wine, white, etc.)
Worcestershire sauce
Salt and pepper

Starches

Bread (pita, sandwich), in freezer
Crackers
Croutons
Dry breadcrumbs

Pasta (egg noodles, macaroni, penne, small shells, spaghetti, etc.)
Rice mixes
Stuffing mix

Personal Items Your Family Uses

Remember, a three-month supply should also include household items like toothpaste, deodorant, and toilet paper. Next week at family home evening, have a brainstorming session with your family to make a list of the items and brands you use. If you have young children, think about items they may need, such as diapers, wipes, diaper-rash cream, and baby wash. This way, you can plan what to buy and won't waste money or space on things your family won't use.

Suggested Personal Items for Three-Month Supply

Dental Hygiene

Toothpaste	Floss
Toothbrushes	Mouthwash

Personal Hygiene

Antibacterial hand soap	Deodorant
Body wash or bar soap	Feminine hygiene products
Shampoo	Toilet paper
Conditioner	

Infant Needs

Diapers	Diaper rash ointment
Wipes	Children's pain reliever & fever reducer
Anti-gas drops	Teething ointments

Medicines

Pain reliever	Hydrocortisone cream
Anti-nausea/anti-diarrhea medication	Antibiotic cream or ointment
Cold/allergy medicine	Bandages

Let the Buying Begin!

Budgeting for Your Three-Month Supply

Now that you have a list of items you need for your three-month-supply, it's time to start shopping. After you buy the groceries you need right now, look at your budget and set aside an amount for your three-month-supply shopping. If you don't have extra money, cut back somewhere else until you have enough to begin building your supply. Remember, it will be worth it, since once you have your three-month supply, you'll be saving a lot of money.

> *Tip: If you don't have money in your budget to start building your three-month supply, try reducing the number of times you eat out as a family. The money you will save by eliminating just one restaurant outing per month could buy a lot of cans of tomato sauce!*

Top 10 Rules for Grocery Shopping

1. When you purchase something you're running out of, buy two. The plan is to always have at least one on hand.

2. Keep your three-month-supply list nearby when you go through grocery ads or coupons. When you see an item from your list on sale, either at the grocery store or with a coupon, stock up.

3. Make a list of items you're running out of, items you need for meals that week, and any three-month-supply items that are on sale or for which you have a coupon. Then take the list with you to the store.

4. Don't go to the grocery store hungry or you'll be tempted to buy items not on your list—items you don't really need.

5. Beware of warehouse bulk buying. Just because you can purchase something in bulk doesn't necessarily mean it is cheaper. Compare prices before you

shop at a warehouse—or anywhere else.

6. If you live in an area where there are case-lot sales, find out when they are and save for them. Again, be sure to compare prices between stores.

7. If you don't know if the price of an item is high or low, watch the price for a couple of weeks.

8. Buy canned foods that look perfect. Torn labels or dust may indicate that the can has been sitting on the shelf for too long. NEVER buy dented or bulging cans, even if they are cheaper. Eating food from a dented or bulging can may lead to botulism, a form of food poisoning that can be fatal.

9. Shop at off-peak times. If you shop late at night or early in the morning during the week, you can often find meat and baked goods at clearance prices. And best of all, the chekout lines will be short!

Putting It to Good Use

Finding Time to Make Dinner

You may be thinking, *This is great, but it doesn't help me find time to make dinner!* Just keep reading. I know that the hour or two before dinner can be the most stressful, with babies fussing and children needing help with their homework. So when should you start dinner? Most people wait to decide what to have for dinner an hour before they want to eat, and by then they're exhausted. Try starting your dinner in the morning or early afternoons, depending on your schedule. If you work during the day, start dinner the night before. Locate the ingredients and do the cutting, mixing, and preparing in advance. Then when it's dinnertime, all you'll need to do is toss something in the oven, combine a few ingredients, and put the meal on the table.

> *Tip: Set the table right after lunch. When it's dinnertime, everyone will think you've prepared dinner—even when you haven't had time yet!*

When to Restock

Since you don't want to run out of anything, you'll need to restock constantly. Keep a list on your refrigerator or in your pantry of the items you use. Then, when the sale ads arrive in your mailbox, you can check to see if anything on your list is on sale. When you see a good deal, act on it. And now that you have an extra of every item, you're saving money because you have time to watch for sales, instead of making an emergency trip to the store to buy that one item at full price.

Tip: Don't let dinner leftovers go to waste! Send them with family members for lunch. Or take a break from cooking one night and create a fun "buffet" with leftovers from several different meals.

Mock Pumpkin Pie, page 147

STEP 3

BUILDING YOUR
ONE-YEAR SUPPLY

STEP 3

BUILDING YOUR
ONE-YEAR SUPPLY

Why Do I Need a One-Year Supply?

Now that you're working on your three-month supply, it's time to talk about a one-year supply. President Thomas S. Monson said, "Many more people could ride out the storm-tossed waves in their economic lives if they had their year's supply of food . . . and were debt-free. Today we find that many have followed this counsel in reverse: they have a year's supply of debt and are food-free" (Thomas S. Monson, "That Noble Gift—Love at Home," *Church News*, May 12, 2001, 7). While President Monson's wonderful sense of humor is reflected in this statement, the point he makes is serious. And although the Church has an expansive storage of food as a part of its welfare program, President Hinckley noted, "The best welfare program is our own welfare program. Five or six cans of wheat in the home are better than a bushel in the [Church's] welfare granary" (Gordon B. Hinckley, "To Men of the Priesthood," *Ensign*, Nov. 2002, 56).

What Should My One-Year Supply Include?

For a one-year supply, the recommended foods are storable long term, high in nutritional value, low in moisture content, and do not require refrigeration. Such foods can sustain life if nothing can be purchased, either due to lack of money or to reduced food supply. Since these foods are also basic ingredients in many recipes, they can easily be rotated along with your three-month supply.

Some Suggested Items for One-Year Supply

Powdered milk	Salt
Powdered eggs	White sugar
Whole wheat	Dried whole beans
Rolled oats	Dried refried beans
White rice	Dried fruits (such as apple slices)
Dried corn	Dried vegetables (such as carrots, potato
Pasta	flakes, and diced onions)
Gluten	Oil and/or shortening

Powdered Milk

Nutritional Value of Milk

Milk is an important part of the American diet. According to the U.S. Department of Agriculture, diets rich in milk and milk products:

- Can help build and maintain bone mass throughout a person's life, helping reduce the risk of osteoporosis.

- Are crucial to bone health during childhood and adolescence, when bone mass is being built.

- Tend to have a higher overall nutritional quality.

- Provide calcium, which the body uses in building bones and teeth and in maintaining bone mass. (Milk products are the primary source of calcium in most American diets.) Diets that provide 3 cups (or the equivalent) of milk products per day can improve bone mass.

- Are rich in potassium, which is necessary for maintaining a healthy blood pressure. Yogurt and fluid milk are rich sources of potassium.

- Provide Vitamin D, which helps the body maintain proper levels of calcium and phosphorous, thereby helping to build and maintain bones. (Milk fortified with vitamin D is a good source of this nutrient.) ("Inside the Pyramid: Milk," USDA; http://www.mypyramid.gov/pyramid/milk_why.html)

Because milk is a complete protein (it has all eight essential amino acids), a carbohydrate, and full of vitamins and minerals, it can be a complete survival meal. In fact, if all you had in your food storage was powdered milk and water, you could survive. (With such great health benefits, why not keep milk around all the time?)

How Powdered Milk Is Made

Powdered milk is made from fresh, pasteurized skim milk. First, the milk is concentrated in an evaporator until 50% of the milk solids remain. Next, the concentrated milk is sprayed into a heated chamber where the water almost instantly evaporates, leaving behind tiny dry milk particles.

Saving Money by Using Powdered Milk

Using powdered milk can save you a lot of money. The current cost of a #10 can of powdered milk at the Church cannery is $7.60. If we divide $7.60 by 5 (the number of gallons of milk in a #10 can), we get $1.68. That's how much a gallon of powdered milk costs. Currently, where I live, the average cost of a gallon of skim milk at the grocery store can cost up to $2.50. Subtracting $1.52 (the cost of a gallon of powdered milk) from $2.50, we get 98 cents. That means that by using powdered milk instead of fresh, I'm saving as much as 98 cents per gallon, based on current prices. And depending on where you live, you may save even more.

Let's say you buy two gallons of milk per week for one year, or 52 weeks. That's 104 gallons of milk per year. Therefore, your annual savings on milk would be $101.92. That's a lot of extra money, and as food prices continue to soar, you can save even more. Even if you don't drink straight powdered milk, you can use it in any recipe calling for milk (or—with modifications—sweetened condensed milk, evaporated milk, or buttermilk), with no negative effect on the taste. (If you've purchased sweetened condensed milk, evaporated milk, or buttermilk lately, you know how expensive they can be.) You'll save money because you'll buy fresh milk for drinking only. For everything else, you'll use that handy (and cheaper) powdered milk.

Where to Buy Powdered Milk

The best place to purchase non-instant powdered milk is an LDS Church cannery. Very few grocery stores sell non-instant powdered milk, and it is difficult to find online. If you do not live near an

LDS cannery, you may want to purchase instant powdered milk. While instant powdered milk is sold at grocery stores, it is usually much less expensive online. Here are some websites that sell instant powdered milk:

> www.emergencyessentials.com
>
> www.honeyvillegrain.com
>
> www.shelfreliance.com

How to Store Powdered Milk

Store powdered milk in tightly sealed containers. Food-safe plastic (PETE) containers, #10 cans, and Mylar®-type bags work best for long-term storage. To preserve quality, use food-safe oxygen absorbers—one per #10 can or two per five- to six-gallon container. (Food-safe oxygen absorbers are available at food-storage supply stores.) Keep powdered milk in a cool, dry place. When stored correctly, powdered milk can last for 20 years or more.

Although the nutrients in powdered milk will last about 20 years if it is stored properly, after 20 years you probably would not want to drink it, as the powder begins to taste stale after about two years in storage. Plus, the older the powdered milk is, the harder it is to mix into water. But if you have old powdered milk that tastes a little funny, don't throw it away, since you can still use it in cooking without a noticeable difference in taste. Just make sure that when you drink powdered milk, you use your newer cans. Clearly, milk is an item you'll want to rotate frequently (see http://providentliving.org/content/display/0,11666,7798-1-4224-1,00.html).

How Much Milk Should I Have in My One-Year Supply?

According to a U.S. government study on maintaining nutritional adequacy during periods of food shortage, you should store 16 pounds of powdered milk for each family member per year (see "Update on Milk Storage," *Ensign*, Mar. 1997, 70–71). The 16 pounds, or 64 quarts, is a minimum suggestion and equates to one small (5- to 6-ounce) glass of milk per day for one family member. (Keep in mind that young children and nursing mothers will need to drink more than one small glass of milk per day, so you'll need to store more for them.) Sixteen pounds per person per year is the bare minimum, and many families will want to store much more.

Action Steps

1. Figure out how much powdered milk your family will need in your one-year supply. Remember, you'll need *at least* 16 pounds, or approximately three #10 cans, per person in your household. *My family will need _____ pounds or _____#10 cans of powdered milk for our one-year supply.*

2. Start purchasing powdered milk for your long-term food storage and for everyday use. If you don't have a Church cannery nearby, you can purchase powdered milk at a local grocery store. However, most grocery stores carry instant powdered milk rather than nonfat dry powdered milk, and you will need to double the amount of nonfat powdered milk called for in most recipes.

3. Compile a list of your family's favorite recipes that use sweetened condensed milk, evaporated milk, white sauce, or milk.

Powdered Eggs

Nutritional Value of Eggs

Eggs are nutrient dense, which means that they provide a lot of nutrition but not a lot of calories. Eating nutrient-dense foods is especially important for young children and older adults. An egg contains essential vitamins and minerals, high-quality protein, healthy unsaturated fats, antioxidants, and only 70 calories. In fact, according to the American Egg Board, there are five major reasons to love eggs:

1. "Weight management: The high-quality protein in eggs helps you feel full longer and stay energized, which contributes to maintaining a healthy weight.

2. Muscle strength and muscle-loss prevention: Research indicates that high-quality protein may help active adults build muscle strength and help prevent muscle loss in middle-aged and aging adults.

3. Healthy pregnancy: Egg yolks are an excellent source of choline, an essential nutrient that contributes to fetal brain development and helps prevent birth defects. One egg provides about 125 milligrams of choline, or roughly one-quarter of the recommended daily intake for pregnant and breastfeeding women.

4. Brain function: Choline also aids the brain function of adults by maintaining

the structure of brain cell membranes, and is a key component of the neurotrans-
mitter that helps relay messages from the brain through nerves to the muscles.

5. Eye health: Lutein and zeaxanthin, two antioxidants found in egg yolks, help
    prevent macular degeneration, a leading cause of age-related blindness. Though
    eggs contain a small amount of these two nutrients, research shows that the
    lutein from eggs maybe more bioavailable than lutein from other food sources."
    ("Cracking the Cholesterol Myth,"; http://incredibleegg.org/health_heart.html)

Cracking the Cholesterol Myth

With all this talk about the wonders of the egg, there is one more issue to deal with: cholesterol. Back
in the 1980s, eggs received a bad rap per their cholesterol content—so bad that some Americans
cut eggs from their diets entirely. But in 2007, the *Medical Science Monitor* reported that based on
a study of 9,500 people, eating one or more eggs a day does not increase the risk of heart disease
or stroke among healthy adults, and that eating eggs may actually be associated with a decrease in
blood pressure (see Qureshi A, et al. Regular egg consumption does not increase the risk of stroke or
cardiovascular diseases. *Medical Science Monitor*. 2007; 13[1]. CR1-8).

How Powdered Eggs Are Made

Powdered eggs were originally created so that military units in the field could always have access
to eggs. Powdered eggs are made from fresh eggs. First, the eggs are washed and then opened. The
liquid egg product is then filtered and chilled, which destroys bacteria such as salmonella. (This
means that you can eat cake batter, brownie batter, and cookie dough again!) Next, the egg product
are dried, usually through a spray-drying process, to create a free-flowing powder.

Saving Money by Using Powdered Eggs

As I'm writing this, the average price of a #10 can of powdered eggs is $19.99. Each can contains
the equivalent of 12½ dozen large eggs, so a "dozen" powdered eggs currently costs $1.60. According
to the American Farm Bureau, during the fourth quarter of 2008 the average cost of a dozen large
eggs was $1.78 (The Voice of Agriculture, "Retail Food Prices Drop Slightly in Last Quarter of
2008," http://www.fb.org/index.php?fuseaction=newsroom.newsfocus&year=2009&file=nr0107.
html). At that price, for each "dozen" powdered eggs you use, you save 18 cents.

Where to Buy Powdered Eggs?

Church canneries do not currently sell powdered eggs, but you should be able to find powdered eggs at a local grocery store that has a preparedness section. Alternately, you can buy powdered eggs at an emergency-preparedness store. If you can't find powdered eggs locally, you can order them online. Here are three websites that carry powdered eggs (these companies also have physical stores, so check first to see if there is one near you):

> www.bluechipgroup.net
>
> www.emergencyessentials.com
>
> www.honeyvillegrain.com

How to Store Powdered Eggs

Store powdered eggs in tightly sealed containers. Food-safe plastic (PETE) containers, #10 cans, and Mylar®-type bags work best for long-term storage. To preserve quality, use food-safe oxygen absorbers—one per #10 can or two per five- to six-gallon container. (Food-safe oxygen absorbers are available at food-storage supply stores.) Keep powdered eggs in a cool, dry place. When stored correctly, powdered eggs can last five to ten years or more.

Powdered eggs are non-perishable and do not need to be stored in the refrigerator, even when the can has been opened. Once opened, powdered eggs need to be used within one year, which is very easy to do.

How Many Cans of Powdered Eggs Should I Have in My One-Year Supply?

Think of how many eggs your family eats in a week, then take that number and multiply it by 52. That is how many eggs your family will eat, on average, in a year. A can of eggs has the equivalent of 216 (about 18 dozen) medium eggs or 150 (about 12½ dozen) large eggs. Take the number of eggs your family will eat in a year and divide it by the number of either medium or large eggs, depending on which size you buy. This should give you a good idea of how many cans you will need in your one-year supply.

Action Steps

1. Figure out how many eggs your family eats in a week, on average. Multiply that number by 52. Then figure out how many cans of eggs your family will

need. Remember, a can of eggs has the equivalent of 216 (about 18 dozen) medium eggs or 150 (about 12½ dozen) large eggs. Take the number of eggs your family will eat in a year and divide it by the number of eggs in a can (either medium or large eggs). *My family will need _____ cans of powdered eggs for our year supply.*

2. Start purchasing powdered eggs for your food storage and to start using today.

3. Compile a list of your family's favorite recipes that use eggs. They can include anything from a brownie mix to French toast.

Whole Wheat

Nutritional Value of Whole Wheat

The truth is, whole wheat is probably the one food storage item that doesn't exist in some other form in your diet—and should. You will love whole wheat because it:

1. Is more nutritious. Whole-wheat flour contains more minerals, vitamins, and natural phytochemicals than does white flour. (See "Inside the Pyramid— Why Is It Important to Eat Grains, Especially Whole Grains?" United States Department of Agriculture; http://www.mypyramid.gov/pyramid/grains_why.html.)

2. Helps with stress. Whole wheat contains B vitamins, which are necessary for healthy nerves. (READ: Eating whole-grain products can help you cope with stress!) (See ibid.)

3. Cleans you out. Whole-wheat foods provide more fiber than do foods made with white flour. Eating more fiber can help prevent constipation, diverticulosis, and many other bowel problems. The Institute of Medicine recommends that a person consume an average of 28 grams of fiber per day, but studies show that the average American consumes only 15 grams. (See "Fiber," American Heart Association; http://www.americanheart.org/presenter.jhtml?identifier=4574.)

4. Helps you lose weight and keep it off! The bounteous fiber in whole wheat has almost no calories, keeps you fuller longer, absorbs three times its weight in water, cuts absorption of calories, cleans out impurities, requires more chewing, takes half as much to fill you up, and takes longer to digest. (See ibid.)

5. Reduces your risk of colon cancer and other diseases (see "Get the Whole Grain Pictures," American Dietetic Association; http://www.eat-right.org/cps/rde/ xchg/ada/hs.xsl/home_4028_ENU_HTML.htm).

6. Can lower your blood pressure, your LDL cholesterol level, and your risk of adult-onset diabetes. Therefore, eating fiber can reduce the number of times you have to visit the doctor and the number of prescriptions you must take, saving you money. (See ibid.)

7. Can cut down on tooth decay, therefore reducing the cost of your dental care (see "Food that Helps Prevent Tooth Decay," Glide; http://www.glidefloss.com/ smart-tips-foods.php).

8. Can cut down on grocery costs because you'll be cooking from scratch. And since whole wheat has more fiber, you and your family will fill up on less food. (See "Slashing your Grocery Bill . . . ," Utah State Extension; http://extension. usu.edu/files/publications/publication/pub__7672180.pdf.)

9. Keeps your body both emotionally and physically used to something that will be a major staple in your diet if you must live off your food storage for a long period of time.

Whole-Wheat Flour Vs. All-Purpose Flour

All-purpose flour, also known as white flour, and whole-wheat flour are made from the same whole-wheat kernel, but in all-purpose flour, the kernel has been stripped of its nutrient-rich germ and reddish-colored bran. All-purpose flour has been "enriched," but of the twenty-two vitamins and minerals stripped from the whole-wheat kernel, only four are added back in. These include iron, thiamin, niacin, and riboflavin. The good news is that you already use flour, and since whole wheat can be ground into flour, it will be simple to start incorporating whole-wheat flour—and its many health benefits—into your diet.

The Difference between Hard Red Wheat and Hard White Wheat

Hard red wheat and hard white wheat are the most common options for long-term food storage. If you grew up eating whole wheat, it was probably the hard red variety, since the hard white wheat only recently became an option for long-term storage. So where did hard white wheat come from? Soft white wheat was used for pastries and baked goods, but because it was soft, it didn't store long term as well as hard wheat. Now, scientists have genetically crossed soft white wheat and hard red wheat to create hard white wheat. The two wheats contain similar amounts of protein and fiber, but they differ in color and taste. Hard red wheat is reddish in color and has a stronger, nuttier flavor. Red wheat makes delicious bread that tastes great with soups and cheese (or anything that tastes good with nuts). Hard white wheat is a golden color and has a more subtle flavor that is easily disguised in baked goods, so if you're worried about taste, use hard white wheat.

Saving Money by Using Whole Wheat

At the present time, 5 pounds of freshly ground whole-wheat flour (the kind I grind myself) costs me about $1.48 to produce. In comparison, all-purpose flour at local grocery stores costs an average of $2.54 for 5 pounds. So, at current prices, grinding my own wheat flour instead of buying all-purpose flour saves me over $1.00 for every 5 pounds I use. In addition, since whole-wheat flour contains fiber and bran, it fills you up faster and takes longer to digest, so your family won't need to eat as much.

If you currently purchase whole-wheat flour, you can save even more money by grinding your own. With a current average price of $3.93 for 5 pounds of whole-wheat flour, compared to $1.48 when I grind it myself, I save well over $2.00 for every 5 pounds I grind myself.

Clearly, you can save a significant amount of money grinding your own whole-wheat flour instead of buying either all-purpose or whole-wheat flour at the grocery store, depending on prices in your area. (To see how much money you could save by grinding your own wheat flour, make the calculations using current flour and wheat prices where you live.)

Where to Buy Whole Wheat

You can purchase hard red wheat at any Church cannery. If you don't live near a Church cannery and can't find wheat elsewhere, you can order hard red wheat from Church Distribution Services at www.ldscatalog.com. Hard white wheat is available for purchase at most grocery stores with an emergency preparedness section.

How to Store Whole Wheat

Store wheat in tightly sealed containers. Food-safe plastic (PETE) containers, #10 cans, and Mylar®-type bags work best for long-term storage. To preserve quality, use food-safe oxygen absorbers—one per #10 can or two per five- to six-gallon container. (Food-safe oxygen absorbers are available at food-storage supply stores.) Keep wheat in a cool, dry place. If stored correctly, wheat can last for 30 years or more.

Grinding Whole Wheat

There are three different types of wheat grinders: hand grinders, electric grinders, and grinders that can be used either way. Hand grinders work without electricity and will definitely give you strong muscles, at least in the arm you use for grinding! Electric grinders obviously won't work if your electricity goes out, but when you do have electricity you can grind wheat much faster with an electric grinder than with a hand grinder. Electric wheat grinders can be messy and loud, so you'll probably want to grind wheat in your garage or outdoors. Wheat grinders can also be used to grind any whole dry grain, i.e., corn, beans, rice, etc.

Wheat grinders run from about $50 (hand grinder) to $450 (electric grinder). It's a good idea to research wheat grinders and decide which fits with your family. (Some companies that sell wheat grinders are K-Tec, Nutrimill, and Grain Mill.)

It's easy to grind wheat and save a lot of money. Give it a try!

How to Store Freshly Ground Wheat

Ground wheat loses its nutritional value very quickly. In addition, ground wheat can go rancid because the wheat germ (the part of the wheat kernel that serves as the seed) contains a small amount of unsaturated fat. Rancid wheat flour has a funny taste that will make it impossible to disguise in your family's favorite recipes. After you grind wheat, cover it tightly and store it in the refrigerator or freezer. Never store ground wheat near foods with strong odors, such as apples and onions, as flour readily absorbs odors. (No one wants an onion-flavored cookie!)

How Much Whole Wheat Should I Have in My One-Year Supply

For a one-year supply, you need about 300 pounds of grains per person. That equates to 25 pounds a month per person. Don't panic—it doesn't need to consist entirely of wheat. The 300 pounds can be divided between wheat, white rice, rolled oats, dried corn, and pasta, according to your family's needs and preferences. However, we focus on whole wheat in this book because most people already know how to use white rice, rolled oats, and pasta, and because dried corn is less versatile than wheat.

Action Steps

1. Figure out how many pounds of wheat and other grains your family will need for your one-year supply. Remember, you'll need 300 pounds per person in your household. *My family will need_____ pounds of wheat and other grains for our one-year supply.*

2. Start purchasing wheat for your one-year supply.

3. Research wheat grinders and decide whether you want a hand grinder, an electric grinder, or a hand-and-electric wheat grinder.

4. Purchase a wheat grinder.

5. If you need to save money for a wheat grinder, borrow one from a friend, neighbor, or family member so that you can learn how to use whole wheat flour while you're saving. Alternately, you can purchase some whole-wheat flour to get you started.

Dried Beans

Nutritional Value of Beans

Beans give you a lot of bang for your buck. They are low in cost, cholesterol free, low in fat (2% to 3%), and high in fiber, protein, carbohydrate, folate, and many trace minerals. In fact, because beans are high in fiber and low in fat, they can actually help lower your cholesterol. According to the Idaho Bean Commission, "Each half-cup serving of dry beans provides six to seven grams of protein, meets at least 10% of the Recommended Dietary Allowance (RDA) for protein, yet costs about 20 cents per serving" ("Nutritional Facts"; http://www2.state.id.us/bean/nutrition/value. htm).

Saving Money by Using Dried Beans

Dried beans are much less expensive than canned beans. With dried beans, it currently costs around 30 cents to make the equivalent of one 15-ounce can of beans. The price of canned beans varies as widely as the types of beans available, but where I live, the least expensive canned beans (pinto) cost around $1.00 per can—and that price can double or triple for organic. Using the lower price ($1.00), you could save around 70 cents for every 15 ounces of beans you make with dried beans. Of course, you always save money using beans as a replacement for meat.

Where to Buy Dried Beans

Dried beans can be purchased at a Church cannery. In fact, some varieties can be purchased from the cannery online at www.ldscatalog.net. Other online options for purchasing dried beans are:

> www.bluechipgroup.net
>
> www.emergencyessentials.com
>
> www.honeyvillegrain.com
>
> www.shelfreliance.com

How to Store Dried Beans

Beans should be stored in tightly sealed containers. Food-safe plastics (PETE) containers, #10 cans, and Mylar®-type bags work best for long-term storage. To preserve bean quality and protect beans from insects, use food-safe oxygen absorbers—one per #10 can or two per five- to six-gallon container. (Food-safe oxygen absorbers are available at food-storage supply stores.) Never store dried beans in the refrigerator. If beans are stored incorrectly, they can absorb water and spoil before you have a chance to use them. When stored correctly, beans can last for 30 years or more.

How Many Pounds of Dried Beans Should I Have in My One-Year Supply?

For a one-year supply, you need about 60 pounds of dried beans or legumes per person per year, or about 5 pounds per month. The Church cannery sells white, black, and pinto beans, which will store for 30 years. The cannery also sells dehydrated refried beans, which can be stored for five to seven years.

Action Steps

1. Figure out how many pounds of beans your family will need for your one-year supply. Remember that you'll need 60 pounds per person in your household. *My family will need _____ pounds of dried beans for our one-year supply.*

2. Start purchasing dried beans for your one-year supply. To start, purchase pinto, white, black, and dehydrated refried beans. (Later, you might want to add other types of dried beans and legumes such as lima beans, garbanzo beans, kidney beans, great northern beans, black-eyed peas, split peas, and lentils.)

3. Compile a list of your family's favorite recipes that use pinto, white, black, or refried beans.

Dried Fruits and Vegetables

Using dried fruits and vegetables instead of fresh eliminates the need to wash, peel, and chop them. And with the dried versions, there is no need to cook fruits and vegetables for long periods of time before using them.

Nutritional Value of Dried Fruits and Vegetables

The good news is that there isn't a significant difference in the nutritional value of dried fruits and vegetables when compared to their fresh counterparts. In the dehydration process, only water has been removed; the vitamins have not been cooked out of the fruits or vegetables.

Eating fruits and vegetables provides enormous health benefits, especially in an emergency. Fruits and vegetables provide nutrients vital for health and maintenance of the body. According to the U.S. Department of Agriculture:

- Eating a diet rich in fruits and vegetables as part of an overall healthy diet may reduce risk for stroke and perhaps other cardiovascular diseases.
- Eating a diet rich in fruits and vegetables as part of an overall healthy diet may reduce risk for type 2 diabetes.
- Eating a diet rich in fruits and vegetables as part of an overall healthy diet may protect against certain cancers, such as mouth, stomach, and colon-rectum cancer.
- Diets rich in foods containing fiber, such as fruits and vegetables, may reduce the risk of coronary heart disease.
- Eating fruits and vegetables rich in potassium as part of an overall healthy diet may reduce the risk of developing kidney stones and may help to decrease bone loss.
- Eating foods such as vegetables that are low in calories per cup instead of some other higher-calorie food may be useful in helping to lower calorie intake." ("Inside the Pyramid—Vegetables"; http://mypyramid.gov/pyramid/vegetables _why.html.)Where to Buy Dried Fruits and Vegetables

Dehydrated apple slices, carrots, onions, and potatoes can be purchased at Church canneries. However, if you want a larger variety of dried fruits and vegetables, some great online options include:

www.bluechipgroup.net

www.emergencyessentials.com

www.honeyvillegrain.com

www.shelfreliance.com

How to Store Dried Fruits and Vegetables

Dehydrated fruits and vegetables should be stored in tightly sealed containers. Food-safe plastic (PETE) containers, #10 cans, and Mylar®-type bags work best for long-term storage. To preserve quality and protect from insects, use food-safe oxygen absorbers—one per #10 can or two per five- to six-gallon container. (Food-safe oxygen absorbers are available at food-storage supply stores.) Dehydrated fruits and vegetables should be stored tightly covered in a cool, dry area. Once opened, they need to be used quickly or placed in smaller, airtight containers so they won't spoil or become soggy due to the humidity in the air. Potato flakes, onions, and apple slices will store unopened for 30 years; carrots will store unopened for 20 years. For other dried fruits and vegetables, check the manufacturer's recommendations.

How Many Cans of Dried Fruits and Vegetables Should I Have in My One-Year Supply?

The amount of dehydrated fruits and vegetables that should be stored is individual to each family. Track how long it takes your family to deplete a #10 can by writing on the label the date you opened the can. Once the can is emptied, determine how long it took, in months, for your family to use the item. Then divide 12 by that number to determine how many cans you would need in your one-year supply.

Action Steps

1. Purchase potato flakes, onion flakes, dehydrated carrots, and dehydrated apple slices. On the label, write the date you open the can. (Later, you may want to conider buying other types of dehydrated vegetables, such as tomatoes, peppers, mushrooms, and celery, and other dehydrated fruits, such as strawberries, bannas,

peaches, and pineapple.)

2. Compile a list of your family's favorite recipes that use mashed potatoes, diced onions or carrots, or apples.

3. Find smaller containers in which to store your dehydrated fruits and vegetables, so that you can keep them in your kitchen cupboards for easy use in cooking and baking.

Overnight Caramel French Toast, page 98

STEP 4

USING POWDERED MILK

STEP 4

USING POWDERED MILK

It's Better Than You Think

Of all the foods that can be stored long term, powdered milk probably gets the worst rap. Most people think that it's difficult to use and that it tastes bad. But today's powdered milk actually tastes much better than what you probably drank as a child. Powdered milk is easy to use (it requires no special tools or cooking preparation), is an easy substitute in recipes calling for milk, and is less messy than fresh milk. Because of its convenience and ease of use, we'll start with powdered milk.

Since you've already completed Step 3, you know where to buy powdered milk, how to store it, and how much you need for your family's one-year supply. Now we will learn about the different types of powdered milk and then actually start using it. (This is getting exciting!) We'll use powdered milk to make sweetened condensed milk, which we'll then use to create delectable desserts. Next, we'll make evaporated milk from powdered milk, and we'll learn to cook with powdered milk. And finally, we'll make drinkable powdered milk.

Difference between Powdered Milk and Milk Alternative Drink Mix

The difference between powdered milk and a milk alternative is similar to the difference between orange juice and Tang: Orange juice is juice that has been extracted from an orange, while Tang is an orange-flavored drink. Powdered milk contains nonfat dry milk, vitamin A palmitate, and vitamin D3. Milk alternative drinks contain sweet dairy whey, nonfat dry milk solids, partially hydrogenated vegetable oil (such as canola oil, soy oil, or both), corn syrup solids, sodium caseinate, dipotassium phosphate, propylene glycol monostearate, monoglycerides and diglycerides, lecithin, carrageenan, Vitamin A, and Vitamin D.

A milk alternative is just that—an alternative drink that isn't milk. The main ingredient in milk alternatives is whey, a byproduct of cheese. Vitamins and minerals are added to make the drink more nutritious. While a milk alternative still costs less than fresh milk, it lacks many of the health benefits of fresh milk. Some people think that a milk alternative tastes better than powdered milk, but powdered milk has come a long way. It's not the same powdered milk that was available fifteen or twenty years ago, and there are many ways to make it taste even better.

The Difference between Instant and Non-Instant Powdered Milk

Instant and non-instant powdered milk are both made from nonfat milk. Once mixed, there is no measurable difference in taste, texture, usability, or nutritional value. The main difference is in the time and effort it takes to dissolve the powder in water for drinking. Dry instant powdered milk is light and fluffy, and it dissolves in cold water with just a few stirs with a spoon, so it can be served right away. Dry non-instant powdered milk is denser, must be dissolved in warm water, and requires more stirring. It should be chilled before it is served.

Non-instant milk takes up less space than instant milk, which is why the Church cannery carries non-instant instead of instant. If you choose to use instant milk, you will need to double the amount of dry non-instant milk called for in the recipes in this book.

All Powdered Milk Is Nonfat

Why Is There No Fat in Powdered Milk?

Fat eventually turns rancid. Therefore, in order to ensure that powdered milk can be stored for long periods of time, all fat is removed from the fresh milk before it is dehydrated.

What Should I Do if I Have Young Children Who Need to Drink Whole Milk?

Powdered milk is valuable for food storage because of its protein content. However, it lacks the fats found in whole milk, which can be important for young children. If you have young children, you may want to consider storing cans of evaporated milk. You'll read more about this later, but evaporated milk was created as a cheaper, more storable version of cream, and it is made from whole milk. Cans of evaporated milk will not store as long as will dry powdered milk, but they will last while you have young children. Another option is to store other high-fat items like peanut butter to supplement your children's fat intake during an emergency.

Sweetened Condensed Milk

Sweetened condensed milk is an easy shortcut to a delectable dessert. It is made from cow's milk with some water removed, with sugar added to inhibit bacterial growth. Sweetened condensed milk was created during the Civil War, to provide soldiers with milk that wouldn't turn rancid on the battlefield. Today, you can use powdered milk to make your own sweetened condensed milk. It's easy; you just blend everything in the blender. And it's so much cheaper—only about 75 cents to make your own "can" of sweetened condensed milk. Once you try it, you'll never go back to buying the kind sold in the stores, which currently costs up to $3.00 per can.

Making Sweetened Condensed Milk from Powdered Milk

Sweetened Condensed Milk

½ c. hot water

1 c. non-instant dry powdered milk

1 c. sugar

1 T. butter

Combine ingredients and mix thoroughly in blender. Use immediately or store in refrigerator or freezer.

Using Homemade Sweetened Condensed Milk in Your Recipes

Here are a few tips for using homemade sweetened condensed milk in your own recipes:

1. Use sweetened condensed milk made from powdered milk in any recipe calling

for canned sweetened condensed milk.

2. Sweetened condensed milk is not the same as evaporated milk and cannot be used interchangeably.

3. An easy way to clean your blender after making sweetened condensed milk is to fill the blender halfway with warm water and add a squirt of dish soap. Blend on low speed until the blender is clean.

Tip: Visit www.everydayfoodstorage.net/videos to watch a video that demonstrates how to make sweetened condensed milk using powdered milk.

Action Steps

On three separate days, try a different recipe with sweetened condensed milk that you have made from powdered milk. You can try some of my favorite recipes or your own. Commit to it by filling in the recipes and dates below.

The three recipes I'll make are:

1._____/Date:_____

2._____/Date:_____

3._____/Date:_____

Recipes Using Sweetened Condensed Milk
Made from Powdered Milk

Sunday Perfect Sundae Pie

This pie is as delicious as ice cream but won't melt. Enjoy!

15 chocolate sandwich cookies,
   crushed (about 1½ c.)

4 T. butter, melted

1 tub (8 oz.) whipped topping,
   thawed, divided

1 c. cold milk (3 T. dry powdered
   milk + 1 c. water)

1 pkg. (4-serving size) vanilla flavor
   instant pudding

2 squares semisweet chocolate,
   melted

⅓ c. canned sweetened condensed
   milk (1½ T. water + 3 T. milk +
3 T. + ⅓ c. sugar + ½ T. butter,
   mixed thoroughly in blender)

Mix cookie crumbs and butter; press firmly onto bottom and up side of 9-inch pie plate. Reserve ½ cup whipped topping. Refrigerate until ready to use. Pour milk into large bowl. Add dry pudding mix. Beat with wire whisk 2 minutes or until well blended. Gently stir in remaining whipped topping. Spoon into crust. Mix melted chocolate and condensed milk until well blended. Spoon over pie. Cut through chocolate mixture several times with knife for marble effect. Freeze 6 hours or until firm. Remove pie from freezer 15 minutes before serving. Let stand at room temperature to soften slightly. Top with reserved whipped topping.

Easy No-Bake Blender Cheesecake

With this cheesecake recipe, there is no mess, and the cheesecake sets up more firmly with homemade sweetened condensed milk than milk from a can.

1 can (14 oz.) sweetened condensed milk (½ c. hot water + 1 c. sugar + 1 c. dry powdered milk + 1 T. butter, thoroughly mixed in blender)

1 pkg. (8 oz.) cream cheese

⅓ c. lemon juice

1 t. vanilla

1 pre-made 9" graham cracker piecrust

1 can pie filling (any flavor you like)

Mix ingredients for sweetened condensed milk in blender. Set blender at low speed and add vanilla, lemon juice, and cream cheese. Gradually increase blender speed until mixture is smooth and creamy, stopping blender once or twice to scrape down the sides. Pour into prepared crust. You'll see the filling start to thicken even as you spread it in the piecrust. Chill 2 hours. (If you're in a hurry, you can place the cheesecake in the freezer for one hour, without changing the properties of the cheesecake.) Top with pie filling and serve. *Tip: Lower-fat cream cheese does not work in this recipe; the cheesecake will not set up.*

Easy Fudge

This classic fudge is scrumptious and turns out perfect every time.

3 c. (18 oz.) semisweet chocolate chips

1 can (14 oz.) sweetened condensed milk (½ c. hot water + 1 c. sugar + 1 c. dry powdered milk + 1 T. butter, mixed thoroughly in blender)

dash salt

1½ t. vanilla extract

⅔ c. chopped nuts, optional

In heavy saucepan over low heat, melt chips in sweetened condensed milk. Remove from heat and stir in remaining ingredients. Spread evenly into an 8-inch square pan lined with waxed paper. Chill in refrigerator for 2 to 3 hours or until firm. Turn fudge onto cutting board and peel off paper, then cut into squares. Store fudge loosely covered at room temperature.

Strawberry Lime Riviera Bars

This tasty dessert combines the sweetness of strawberries with the tartness of lime.

1¼ c. finely crushed pretzels

6 T. butter or margarine, melted

1 can (14 oz.) sweetened condensed milk (½ c. hot water + 1 c. sugar + 1 c. dry powdered milk + 1 T. butter, mixed thoroughly in blender)

1 c. puréed strawberries

½ c. lime juice

1 tub (8 oz.) whipped topping, thawed

Mix crushed pretzels and butter in 9x13-inch pan; press firmly into bottom of pan. Refrigerate until ready to use. In a medium bowl, combine strawberries, sweetened condensed milk, and lime juice, mixing well. Gently stir in whipped topping, then pour mixture evenly over crust. Place in freezer for at least 6 hours. Remove from freezer 15 minutes before serving. Let stand at room temperature to soften slightly before cutting in squares. Store leftovers in freezer.

7-Layer Bars

This dessert is a classic and a favorite at our house. It is so easy to make!

½ c. (1 stick) butter

1½ c. crushed graham crackers

1 c. flaked coconut

1 c. (6 oz.) chocolate chips

1 c. (6 oz.) butterscotch chips

1 can (14 oz.) sweetened condensed milk (½ c. hot water + 1 c. sugar + 1 c. dry powdered milk + 1 T. butter, mixed thoroughly in blender)

1 c. walnuts or pecans, chopped

As you preheat the oven, melt butter in an 8½x11-inch pan in the oven. Remove pan from oven and add remaining ingredients in order listed, layer by layer (do not mix). Bake for 32 minutes at 350º F in an aluminum pan, or 28 minutes at 350º F in a glass dish. (Time baking carefully.) Cut into bars when cool.

Easy No-Bake Blender Cheesecake, page 66

Evaporated Milk

When you think of evaporated milk, you probably think of that classic pumpkin pie you make for Thanksgiving. Canned evaporated milk was invented during the Great Depression as a substitute for cream in cooking, and as a way to store milk longer. In fact, my grandmother grew up putting evaporated milk in her cereal and still prefers the taste to that of regular milk. Evaporated milk is homogenized milk with 60% of the water removed. Evaporated milk can be used to make delicious confections such as fudge, caramel dip, cakes, hot fudge sauce, and of course, pumpkin pie.

Since most recipes call for one 12-ounce can of evaporated milk, I've made it easy for you!

Evaporated Milk

1½ c. water

½ c. + 1 T. dry non-instant powdered milk

Combine ingredients and mix well before using in a your recipe. Yield: 1½ cups—the quivalent of a 12-oz. can.

Tips for Using Homemade Evaporated Milk in Your Recipes

1. Use evaporated milk made from powdered milk in any recipe calling for canned evaporated milk, cream (if you aren't going to whip it), half-and-half, or whole milk.

2. Evaporated milk is not the same as sweetened condensed milk and cannot be used interchangeably.

3. Save a dish! Using a 2- or 4-cup liquid measuring cup, measure the amount of water you need. Then just add the dry powdered milk to the water and mix it right in the measuring cup.

Action Steps

On three separate days, try a different recipe with evaporated milk that you made from powdered milk. You can try some of my favorite recipes or your own. Commit to it by filling in the recipes and dates below.

The three recipes I'll make are:

1._____/Date:_____

2._____/Date:_____

3._____/Date:_____

Rocky Road Fudge, page 70

Favorite Recipes Using Evaporated Milk
Made from Powdered Milk

Hard-Shell Ice Cream Sauce

This sauce is expensive to buy at the store, so why not make it at home and save money?

2 c. semisweet chocolate chips

½ c. butter, cut into chunks

⅓ c. evaporated milk (2 T. dry
     powdered milk + ⅓ c. water)

vanilla ice cream

½ cup sliced almonds (optional)

In a heavy saucepan, combine chocolate chips, butter, and milk. Cook over low heat, stirring constantly, until chips are melted and mixture is smooth. Serve warm over ice cream (sauce will harden). Sprinkle with almonds. Refrigerate any leftovers. Sauce can be reheated in the microwave. Yield: about 2 cups.

Rocky Road Fudge

This candy is simple to make but tastes like you spent all day in the kitchen.

4½ c. sugar

1 can (12 oz.) evaporated milk (½ c. +
     1 T. dry powdered milk +
     1½ c. water)

4 C. (8 sticks) butter

1 jar (8 oz.) marshmallow cream

2½ c. chopped nuts

3 c. chocolate chips

1½ t. vanilla

dash salt

4 c. miniature marshmallows

Boil evaporated milk and sugar for 2 minutes over low heat, stirring occasionally. Remove from heat and let cool for 3 minutes. In large container, pour milk/sugar mixture over butter, marshmallow cream, chopped nuts, chocolate chips, vanilla, and salt. Stir until combined and chocolate is melted. Stir in marshmallows. Pour mixture into two 9x13-inch pans and refrigerate for 2 to 4 hours or until firm.

Cheeseburger Meat Loaf

If your family isn't a big fan of meat loaf, try this one. They'll love it!

  1½ lb. ground beef

  1 t. salt

  ⅛ t. pepper

  ⅛ t. thyme

  ½ c. evaporated milk (3 T. dry
      powdered milk + ½ c. water)

  1 egg

  1½ c. soft breadcrumbs

  ½ medium onion, finely chopped

  ¾ to 1 c. cheddar cheese, cubed

Sprinkle meat with seasonings and toss with fork to distribute. Combine egg and milk in mixing bowl and stir in crumbs. Add ground beef and remaining ingredients. Mix lightly until blended. Bake at 350° F for 65 minutes.

Caramel-Marshmallow Dip

Try this dip with fruit, graham crackers, or cookies.

  4 c. miniature marshmallows

  25 caramels (about half of a 14-oz. bag)

  ¼ c. evaporated milk (1½ T. dry
      powdered milk + ¼ c. water)

Place marshmallows, caramels, and evaporated milk in a *large* microwavable bowl and microwave on HIGH for 2 minutes. (Put a paper towel under the bowl to catch any spills, as it can boil over.) Stir. Microwave 1 more minute or until marshmallows are completely melted. Stir mixture until well blended. Cool slightly. Serve warm as a dip.

No-Bake Lime Cheesecake

This creamy cheesecake has a nice citrus kick.

  1 pkg. (8 oz.) cream cheese, softened

  1 large package (6 oz.) lime gelatin

  ⅓–½ c. sugar

  ¾ can (1 c. + 1 T.) evaporated milk
      (4½ T. dry powdered milk +
      ¾ c. water)

  9-inch prepared graham cracker crust

  1 t. vanilla

  whipped topping

Mix gelatin and 1 cup boiling water. When dissolved, add 10 or 12 ice cubes. Then place in refrigerator or freezer until firm but not frozen. Mix cream cheese, sugar, vanilla, and evaporated milk. When gelatin is set firm, add to this mixture and beat until smooth. (Mixture will thicken quickly.) Pour mix into graham cracker crust, then chill pie for at least 30 minutes. Serve with whipped cream or whipped topping.

Caramel Apples

A favorite treat for fall.

   1 c. white sugar

   ½ c. brown sugar

   ⅓ c. butter

   ⅓ c. corn syrup

   ½ c. evaporated milk (3 T. dry

      powdered milk + ½ c. water)

   ½ t. salt

   1 t. vanilla

   6–8 medium Granny Smith apples

   8 sticks or spoons

Cook all ingredients, except vanilla, until caramel forms and is firm and stretchy (about 240° F on a candy thermometer). Remove from heat and add vanilla. When caramel has cooled slightly, dip apples. If caramel becomes too think for dipping, reheat it over low heat or use a double boiler.

Rice Pudding

A great dessert made from your pantry!

   ⅓ c. rice, uncooked

   ⅓ c. sugar

   3 c. evaporated milk (1 c. + 2 T. dry

      powdered milk + 3 c. water)

   1–2 t. cinnamon to taste

   1 tsp. vanilla

   nutmeg

   ¼ c. raisins (optional)

Preheat oven to 350° F. Combine all ingredients except nutmeg and pour into 1½-quart baking dish. Sprinkle nutmeg over top. Bake for 1 hour to 1 hour 15 minutes, stirring every 15 minutes.

Hard-Shell Ice Cream Sauce, page 70

Magic Mix

If you've ever tried to make a white sauce, you know it can be a little tricky. With Magic Mix, making white sauce is simple and quick, and you'll use your powdered milk. So say hello to Magic Mix and perfect white sauces in seconds!

Developed by the Utah State Extension Service, Magic Mix is a combination of powdered milk, butter, and flour. Once you use it to make a white sauce, Magic Mix will be the new "must have" in your cooking arsenal. Try these recipes (or any recipes that call for a white sauce), and your family won't be able to resist! (see "Don't Waste Your Dry Milk," Utah State Extension; http://extension. usu.edu/files/publications/publication/pub__5009141.pdf).

Recipe for Magic Mix

Magic Mix

2⅓ c. dry powdered milk

1 c. all-purpose flour, or ½ c. cornstarch

1 c. (2 sticks) butter, at room temperature

Combine dry milk, flour or cornstarch, and butter into a large bowl. Mix with electric hand mixer until it looks like cornmeal. Keep mix tightly covered in the refrigerator for up to eight months. Yield: 5 cups.

How to Use Magic Mix

It's simple! Just use Magic Mix in any recipe calling for a white sauce. Some dishes that often contain a white sauce are creamy soups, homemade macaroni and cheese, pasta sauces, and vegetable dishes like new potatoes with peas.

Magic Mix White Sauce

⅔ c. Magic Mix

1 c. water

In saucepan, combine Magic Mix and water. Stir rapidly (I use a wire whisk) over medium heat until mixture starts to bubble and thicken. Yield: 1 cup.

Tip: Visit www.everydayfoodstorage.net/videos to watch a video that demonstrates how to make Magic Mix.

Magic Mix Gravy

⅔ c. Magic Mix

1 c. meat drippings and water or broth

In a saucepan, combine Magic Mix with meat drippings and water or broth. Stir rapidly with a wire whisk over medium heat until the mixture starts to bubble and thicken. Salt and pepper to taste.

Action Steps

On three separate days, try a different recipe with a white sauce or gravy made from Magic Mix. You can try some of my favorite recipes or your own. Commit to it by filling in the recipes and dates below.

The three recipes I'll make with Magic Mix are:

1._____/Date:_____

2._____/Date:_____

3._____/Date:_____

Favorite Recipes Using Magic Mix

Magic Mix Fudgsicles

These fudgsicles are super easy, delicious, and great portion control . . . if you can stop at just one!

½ c. sugar

1 c. Magic Mix

2–3 T. cocoa (optional)

2 c. water

1 t. vanilla

½ c. milk

In saucepan, combine Magic Mix, sugar, and cocoa and mix well. Add water, then stir over medium heat until pudding bubbles. Beat in vanilla. Add ½ cup milk (1½ T. powdered milk + ½ c. water) to pudding and stir. Pour into ice-cube trays with toothpicks or small paper cups with spoons. (If using ice-cube trays, cover filled trays with aluminum foil and then insert toothpicks.)

Magic Mix Pudding

If you've never liked pudding, you will when you try this recipe.

½ c. sugar

1 c. Magic Mix

2–3 T. cocoa

2 c. water

1 t. vanilla

Combine Magic Mix, sugar, and cocoa in saucepan and mix well. Add water and stir over medium heat until pudding bubbles. Beat in vanilla. Cover and cool.

Pesto Alfredo Sauce

You won't believe how easy—and inexpensive—it is to make this sauce.

⅔ c. Magic Mix

1 c. water

1 c. Parmesan cheese (if you use canned
  it will be thicker)

½ c. pesto

dash salt

dash pepper

In a saucepan, combine Magic Mix and water. Stir rapidly over medium heat until mixture starts to bubble. Add Parmesan cheese, pesto, salt, and pepper. Serve warm over hot noodles.

Condensed Cream of Chicken Soup

This soup is easy to make and tastes much better than the canned version.

1 c. Magic Mix

¾ c. chicken broth

1 t. dried parsley flakes (optional)

dash onion salt

Combine Magic Mix and chicken broth. Stir constantly over medium-high heat until mixture

thickens. Add parsley and a dash of onion salt. Use in any recipe calling for canned cream of chicken soup.

Tip: Visit www.everydayfoodstorage.net/ videos to watch a video that demonstrates how to make condensed cream of chicken soup from Magic Mix.

Condensed Cream of Mushroom Soup

Try this soup on its own or in recipes that call for condensed cream of mushroom soup.

1 c. Magic Mix

1 can (4.5 oz.) mushroom pieces and
  stems, undrained

¼ c. water

2 drops Kitchen Bouquet® (optional,
  for color only)

dash onion salt

dash pepper

Combine Magic Mix, mushrooms and liquid, and water. Stir constantly over medium-high heat until mixture thickens. Add Kitchen Bouquet®, onion salt, and pepper. Use in any recipe calling for canned cream of mushroom soup.

Condensed Cream of Broccoli Soup

I use this to make a creamy potato broccoli-potato soup.

1 c. Magic Mix

¾ c. water from cooking broccoli

1 c. chopped broccoli, cooked and
    drained

½ t. onion powder

dash garlic salt

Combine Magic Mix and water from cooking broccoli. Stir constantly over medium-high heat until mixture thickens. Add broccoli, onion powder, and garlic salt. Use in any recipe calling for canned cream of broccoli soup.

Condensed Cream of Celery Soup

For an amazing tuna casserole, substitute this easy soup for the canned version.

1 c. Magic Mix

¾ c. water from cooking celery

1 c. chopped celery, cooked and drained

pinch celery seed

1 t. dry parsley flakes (optional)

Combine Magic Mix and water from cooking the celery. Stir constantly over medium-high heat until mixture thickens. Add celery, celery salt, and parsley. Use in any recipe calling for canned cream of celery soup.

Condensed Cream of Tomato Soup

This soup tastes wonderful with a grilled cheese sandwich.

1 c. Magic Mix

1 15-oz. can diced tomatoes

1 t. dried parsley flakes (optional)

dash salt

dash pepper

Combine Magic Mix and diced tomatoes. Stir constantly over medium-high heat until mixture thickens. Add parsley and a dash of salt and pepper. Blend in blender until smooth. Serve immediately, or use in any recipe calling for canned cream of tomato soup.

Cooking with Powdered Milk

Now that you know how to use powdered milk to replace certain ingredients in desserts and white sauces, it's time to take the next step: substituting powdered milk in recipes that call for milk. You'll save money, and you'll save that expensive fresh milk for drinking.

The most complicated part about substituting powdered milk for fresh milk is figuring out how much powdered milk and water you'll need, since only quart measurements are given on a package of powdered milk. But there's no need to fear—I've broken it down for you in an easy-to-read chart. Remember that if you're using instant powdered milk, you will need to double the amount of dry non-instant milk called for in a recipe.

Milk Conversion Chart

Milk Needed	Water	Dry Non-Instant Powdered Milk
1 cup	1 cup	3 tablespoons
¾ cup	¾ cup	2¼ tablespoons
⅔ cup	⅔ cup	2 tablespoons
½ cup	½ cup	1½ tablespoons
⅓ cup	⅓ cup	1 tablespoon
¼ cup	¼ cup	¾ tablespoon

Tips for Using Dry Powdered Milk as a Substitute for Milk in Everyday Cooking

1. Save a dish. You don't need to mix the dry powdered milk and water before adding them to the other ingredients. Use powdered milk in any recipe calling for milk by adding the dry powdered milk to the dry ingredients, and the necessary water to the wet ingredients.

2. Skip a step. You don't have to scald powdered milk. Use powdered milk instead of scalded milk in any recipe calling for scalded milk—without scalding!

3. Make your own cooking substitute for buttermilk. Add 1 tablespoon of white vinegar or lemon juice to 1 cup mixed powdered milk and let stand for five minutes before adding to your recipe.

> *Tip: If you want to print a conversion chart, visit my website at www. everydayfoodstorage.net/download-handouts, then download the "Powdered Milk Conversion Chart."*

Action Steps

On three separate days, try a different recipe where you substitute powdered milk for fresh milk. A great place to start is with mixes, i.e., cornbread, muffin, or pudding. You can try some of my favorite recipes or your own. Commit to it today by filling in the recipes and dates below.

The three recipes I'll make by substituting powdered milk for fresh milk are:

1._____/Date:_____

2._____/Date:_____

3._____/Date:_____

Favorite Recipes Using Powdered Milk

Easy Pasta Pizza

This fun twist on traditional pizza is perfect for both children and adults.

8 oz. spaghetti, cooked, drained

1 egg, beaten

¼ c. milk (¾ T. dry powdered milk + ¼ c. water)

½ lb. extra-lean ground beef

1 can (14 oz.) tomato sauce

1 envelope garlic & herb dressing mix

1 c. mozzarella cheese

Toss spaghetti, egg, and milk in large bowl. Spread evenly in greased 12-inch pizza pan. Brown meat in medium skillet; drain. Stir in tomato sauce and dressing mix. Spoon over spaghetti crust. Sprinkle with cheese. Bake at 350° F for 20 to 25 minutes or until cheese is melted.

Ultra Creamy Cheese Dip

You'll love this tasty update of an old classic.

1 tub (8 oz.) ⅓ less-fat cream cheese (Philadelphia® brand works well)

¼ c. milk (¾ T. dry powdered milk + ¼ c. water)

1 pkg. (8 oz.) shredded sharp cheddar cheese

½ c. red peppers, chopped

1 green onion, sliced

crackers (I like Wheat Thins®)

Beat cream cheese and milk with mixer until well blended. Add cheddar cheese; mix well. Stir in peppers and onions. Refrigerate several hours or until chilled. Serve with crackers.

Ultimate Banana Cream Pie Bars

This decadent dessert always leaves everyone asking for more.

- 1½ c. vanilla wafers, crushed (about 60 wafers)
- ½ c. chopped pecans
- ⅓ c. butter or margarine, melted
- 3 bananas, sliced
- 3 c. cold milk (½ c. + 1 T. dry powdered milk + 3 c. cold water)
- 2 pkgs. (4 servings each) vanilla flavor instant pudding
- 2½ cups thawed whipped topping, divided

Preheat oven to 325° F. Mix wafer crumbs, pecans, and butter in 9x13-inch baking dish; press firmly into bottom of dish. Bake 8 minutes. Remove from oven and place on cooling rack for 10 minutes. Top crust with banana slices. Pour milk into large bowl. Add pudding mixes. Beat with wire whisk 2 minutes or until well blended. Spoon 2 cups of pudding over banana layer. Gently stir 1 cup of whipped topping into remaining pudding; spoon over pie. Top with remaining 1½ cups whipped topping. Refrigerate 3 hours. Store any leftovers in refrigerator.

Simple Powdered-Sugar Icing

So easy, so delicious!

- 2 c. powdered sugar
- 3 T. milk (½ T. dry powdered milk + 3 T. water)

Mix powdered sugar and milk until well blended. Makes about 1 cup of icing.

Company Ham Casserole

This casserole is a great way to use leftover ham.

- ½ c. salad dressing
- ¼ c. milk (¾ T. dry powdered milk + ¼ c. water)
- 1½ c. rotini pasta, cooked, drained
- 2 c. broccoli florets
- 1½ c. coarsely chopped ham
- ½ green or red pepper, chopped
- 1½ cups cheddar cheese, divided
- seasoned croutons (optional)

Mix dressing and milk in large bowl. Add pasta, broccoli, ham, peppers, and 1 cup cheese; mix lightly. Spoon into a 1½-quart casserole. Sprinkle with remaining ½ cup cheese. Bake at 350° F for 30 minutes or until thoroughly heated. Sprinkle with croutons.

Pecan-Crusted Salmon

A delicious combination of sweet and crunchy perfectly complements fresh or frozen salmon.

4 salmon fillets (about 6 oz. each)

2 c. milk (⅓ c. dry powdered milk + 2 c. water)

1 c. finely chopped pecans

½ c. all-purpose flour

¼ c. packed brown sugar

2 t. seasoned salt

2 t. pepper

3 T. vegetable oil

Place salmon fillets in a large zipper-top plastic bag; add milk. (Mix powdered milk together first.) Seal bag and turn to coat. Let stand for 10 minutes; drain. Meanwhile, in a shallow bowl, combine pecans, flour, brown sugar, seasoned salt, and pepper. Coat fillets with pecan mixture, gently pressing it into the fish.

In a large skillet, brown salmon in oil over medium-high heat. Transfer to a 10x15-inch baking pan coated with nonstick cooking spray. Bake at 400° F for 8 to 10 minutes or until fish flakes easily with a fork. Serve with mashed sweet potatoes and fresh vegetables.

Chocolate Lover's Easy Mousse

This smooth confection will make your mouth happy!

1½ c. cold milk, divided (4½ T. dry powdered milk + 1½ c. milk, chilled)

2 squares semisweet baking chocolate

1 pkg. (4-serving size) instant chocolate pudding

2 c. whipped topping, divided

Microwave 1 cup milk and chocolate squares in large microwaveable bowl for 2 minutes; stir until chocolate is melted. Add remaining milk and dry pudding mix, then beat for 2 minutes. Refrigerate for 20 minutes. Whisk in 1½ cups whipped topping; spoon into 6 dessert dishes. Place dollops of whipped topping on top of mousse.

Easy Pasta Pizza, page 80

Making Drinkable Powdered Milk

Now that you know your family will eat desserts and other dishes that contain powdered milk, it's time to try *drinking* powdered milk. It's important to do this now, to find out how your family will drink their powdered milk before you need to use it. Then you can use it if you run out of regular milk and can't get to the store, or if you need to cut your food budget without sacrificing nutrition. Instead of immediately serving powdered milk at every meal, start with treats like smoothies or hot chocolate, then try it on cereal. Finally, give your family members a glass of milk without telling them it's powdered.

Your homework is to find the tricks that will get your family drinking powdered milk. In my house we drink only powdered milk (we eased our way into it), and we save a lot of money by doing so.

Tips for Drinking Powdered Milk

1. Use it first in something where there are other flavors. Try it in chocolate milk, in a milk shake, or on cereal.

2. Mix liquid powdered milk with equal amounts of whole or 2% fresh milk. Mixing it with whole milk will create the equivalent of 2% milk, and mixing it with 2% milk will make the equivalent of 1% milk.

3. For better flavor, add ½ teaspoon vanilla and 1½ teaspoon sugar to 1 gallon of powdered milk.

4. For easy mixing and storage of liquid powdered milk, use a 1-gallon jug. Sterilite's 1-gallon jug has a handle, a slim design that lets you put it in you refrigerator door, and a lid with a closeable spout.

Drinkable Powdered Milk

3 c. dry powdered milk

1 gallon water

1½ t. sugar (optional)

½ t. vanilla (optional)

Place half the water in a 1-gallon jug or pitcher. Add dry powdered milk, then mix with a wire whisk. Add sugar and/or vanilla. Slowly add the rest of the water and mix again. At this point, the milk will be frothy, so you may not be able to fit all the water in the jug. Just remember to add a little more water to the milk before serving.

You *must* serve the milk chilled. There is nothing worse than warm powdered milk!

Don't Just Take My Word for It

Here are some of the comments I've received about powdered milk on my website.

"I was making a smoothie today with frozen fruit, yogurt, and milk. I had already started before realizing my milk had expired . . .Thanks to you, I thought of putting powdered milk in it instead. Well, I'm sure you already know this, but it turned out just as good—well, better because I don't have to worry about powdered milk going bad."

–Julie W.

"I drink my powdered milk all of the time now and was SHOCKED when I had a group of nine- and ten-year-old girls over at my house eating cookies and drinking my powdered milk! I never told them that I was serving them powdered milk, and they never noticed that my milk jug was different. In fact, they commented on how delicious the milk was and had seconds and thirds! " – Amelia F.

Action Steps

Try making drinkable powdered milk three separate times. You can make your family's favorite kind of chocolate milk, or make a milk shake or smoothie. Below are some recipes that make powdered milk more palatable. Commit to using your powdered milk by filling in the recipes and dates below.

The three recipes I'll make with powdered milk are:

1._____/Date:_____

2._____/Date:_____

3._____/Date:_____

Favorite Drinks Recipes Using Powdered Milk

Banana Freeze

This recipe makes good use of the juice from canned pineapple.

1 c. unsweetened pineapple juice

½ medium banana, cut into 1-inch

pieces

2 t. dry powdered milk

1 c. ice cubes

Place ingredients in blender jar in order listed. Place cover on blender jar. Turn blender on using the CRUSHED ICE setting, blending until mixture is smooth. Variation: Omit ice cubes and use 1 c. frozen strawberries. Makes two 8-ounce servings.

Cheater's Hot Chocolate

This hot chocolate tastes so similar to the old-fashioned kind, you'll feel like you're cheating when you make it!

6 c. milk (1 c. + 2 T. dry powdered milk

+ 6 c. water)

1 pkg. (4-servings) chocolate instant

pudding

6 T. whipped topping, thawed

Pour milk into medium saucepan. Add dry pudding mix; beat with wire whisk for 1 minute. Bring just to simmer on medium heat, stirring frequently with wire whisk. Pour evenly into six mugs; top with whipped topping.

Cookie Milk Shake

No one can turn down this delightful milk shake!

12 chocolate sandwich cookies (I use
　　Oreos®)

1½ c. milk (4 ½ T. dry powdered milk +
　　1½ c. water)

1 pt. (2 cups) vanilla ice cream, softened

¼ c. chocolate syrup

Chop or coarsely break cookies. Place milk, ice cream, and chocolate syrup in blender container. Add chopped cookies; cover. Blend on high speed until smooth. Pour into 4 glasses. Serve immediately.

Chocolate Milk

Your family will never know this delicious treat is made with powdered milk.

1 qt. water

¾ c. dry powdered milk

½ c. chocolate milk mix (Nesquik® is
　　my favorite)

Mix dry ingredients together first, then mix with water. Chill before serving.

Make-Ahead Milk Shakes

Since these luscious shakes don't contain ice cream, they won't melt in the fridge.

3½ c. milk (½ c. + 2½ T. dry powdered
　　milk + 3½ c. water)

1 pkg. (4-serving size) vanilla instant
pudding (can use sugar-free)

1 medium ripe banana, cut into chunks

½ c. strawberries

Place all ingredients in blender and blend for 1 minute. Refrigerate until ready to serve. Yield: 4 milk shakes.

Banana Freeze, page 85

STEP 5

USING POWDERED EGGS

STEP 5

USING POWDERED EGGS

An Egg-cellent Way to Use to Food Storage

You're now using powdered milk in your cooking and baking. Now it's time to learn to use powdered eggs. In this step, you'll start replacing fresh eggs with powdered eggs when you bake, then learn how to make exceptional breakfasts with powdered eggs. Finally, you'll learn how to extend fresh eggs with powdered eggs.

Be sure to keep cooking with powdered milk as you're learning to use powdered eggs. Many recipes in this step contain both powdered milk and powdered eggs. We're building step-by-step so that by time you finish this book, it will be second nature for you to cook with your food storage—every day.

Baking with Powdered Eggs

We'll start by substituting powdered eggs for fresh eggs in baking. This is the perfect way to introduce them to your family. No one can taste the difference, and using powdered eggs helps stretch your fresh eggs, saving you money. And with powdered eggs, you can easily halve a recipe calling for one egg.

Now when you make cookies and other baked desserts that contain eggs, your kids can lick the bowl! No more picking eggshells out of the batter, no more salmonella scares, and no more eggs breaking on the floor. Start using powdered eggs today—you'll love them.

one medium egg = 1 T. dry powdered egg + 2 T. water

one large egg = 1½ T. dry powdered egg + 3 T. water

one extra large egg = 2 T. dry powdered egg + ¼ c. water

Tips for Using Powdered Eggs in Your Baking Recipes

1. Use powdered eggs in any baking recipe that calls for eggs.

2. Save a dish. You don't need to mix the dry powdered eggs with water before you add them to the other ingredients. Just add the dry egg powder to the dry ingredients, and the necessary water to the wet ingredients.

3. Make it easy to measure. Don't count out more than two tablespoons for either dry powdered eggs or water; use a measuring cup instead. (There are 16 tablespoons in one cup.) Here is an easy conversion chart.

    2 tablespoons = ⅛ cup
    4 tablespoons = ¼ cup
    6 tablespoons = ⅓ cup
    8 tablespoons = ½ cup
    10 tablespoons = ⅔ cup
    12 tablespoons = ¾ cup

Action Steps

On three separate days, try a different baking recipe where you substitute powdered eggs for fresh eggs. You can try some of my favorite recipes or your own. Commit to it today by filling in the recipes and dates below.

The three baking recipes I'll make using powdered eggs are:

1._____/Date:_____

2._____/Date:_____

3._____/Date:_____

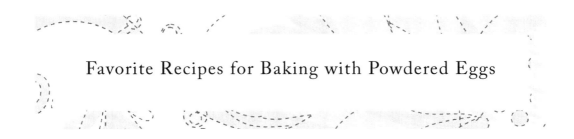

Favorite Recipes for Baking with Powdered Eggs

Sugar Cookies

These cookies are even more fun to make when you enlist your children's help.

¾ c. shortening

1 c. sugar

2 eggs (2 T. dry powdered eggs + ¼ c. water)

½ t. lemon flavoring or vanilla

2½ c. flour

1 t. baking powder

1 t. salt

Throughly mix shortening, sugar, eggs, and flavoring. Stir flour, baking powder, and salt together; blend with wet mixture. Chill dough for 1 hour. Heat oven to 450° F. Roll dough ⅛-inch thick on lightly floured board. Cut with 3-inch cookie cutter. Bake for 6 to 8 minutes.

Peanut Butter Fudge Bars

If you like peanut butter and chocolate, this is the dessert for you!

1 pkg. (18.25 oz.) yellow cake mix

1 c. creamy peanut butter

1 extra large egg (2 T. dry powdered eggs + ¼ c. water)

¼ c. vegetable oil

1 can (14 oz.) sweetened condensed milk (1 c. dry powdered milk, 1 c. sugar, ½ c. hot water, 1 T. butter, thoroughly mixed in blender)

1 c. (6 oz.) semisweet chocolate chips

In a bowl, use a wire whisk to thoroughly combine the cake mix, peanut butter, and egg. Press two-thirds of the mixture into a greased 9x13-inch baking pan. Bake at 350° F for 10 minutes, then cool for 5 minutes. Heat the milk, chocolate chips, and butter over low heat in heavy saucepan. Stir until blended and pour over crust. Sprinkle with remaining crumb mixture. Bake for 20 to 25 minutes or until golden brown. Cool on a wire rack. Cut into bars.

Tropical Hawaiian Cake

When you try this cake, you will say, "Aloha!"

> 1 pkg. (18.25 oz.) yellow cake mix
>
> 1 c. water
>
> ⅓ c. oil
>
> 3 extra large eggs (⅓ c. dry powdered
> eggs + ⅔ c. water)
>
> 1½ c. milk (¼ c. + 1 T. dry powdered
> milk + 1½ c. water)
>
> ½ c. sugar
>
> 2 c. coconut, divided
>
> 1 tub (8 oz.) whipped topping, thawed
>
> 1 can (20 oz.) pineapple chunks,
> drained

Preheat the oven to 350° F. Blend ingredients in large bowl at low speed until moistened—about 3 seconds. Beat at medium speed for 2 minutes. Pour batter in pan and bake immediately. (Check cake-mix box for specific baking times.) After removing from oven, cool cake in pan for 15 minutes. Pierce cake with fork at ½-inch intervals.

Combine milk, sugar, and ½ cup coconut in medium saucepan. Bring to boil on medium heat. Reduce heat to low; simmer 1 minute, stirring occasionally. Spoon over warm cake; spread coconut to evenly cover top of cake. Cool completely. Add ½ cup of remaining coconut to whipped topping; stir gently until well blended. Spread over cake. Sprinkle with remaining 1 cup coconut. Refrigerate 6 hours or overnight. Top with pineapple.

Chocolate Raspberry Cake

This cake tastes so gourmet that everyone will think you bought it at an expensive bakery.

> 1 pkg. (18.25 oz.) devil's food cake mix
>
> 1 c. puréed pumpkin or yellow squash
>
> ½ c. water
>
> 2 T. vegetable oil
>
> 3 large eggs (or 4½ T. dry powdered
> eggs + ½ c. + 1 T. water)
>
> ¾ c. sour cream
>
> ½–¾ c. red raspberry jam
>
> chocolate frosting

Preheat the oven to 350° F. In a large bowl, mix the cake mix, yellow squash or pumpkin purée, water, oil, eggs, and sour cream. Beat until smooth, 1 to 2 minutes.

Divide batter between two 8-inch round cake

pans and bake for 30 to 35 minutes or until toothpick inserted in the middle comes out clean. Cool in pans on cooling racks for five minutes before removing cakes from pans. Cool completely.

Mix ½ cup raspberry jam with ½ cup chocolate frosting. Cover the top of one cake layer with this frosting mixture. Then place the second layer on top and frost the entire cake with plain chocolate frosting. To dress up the cake, place fresh raspberries on top of the cake and dust with powdered sugar.

German Chocolate Brownies

These rich brownies almost melt in your mouth, and, they taste even better than traditional German chocolate cake.

1 pkg. (19.5 oz.) brownie mix

¼ c. water

⅔ c. oil

2 eggs (2 T. dry powdered eggs + ¼ c. water)

¼ c. butter, cut up

4 oz. cream cheese, cubed

½ c. brown sugar

1 c. flaked coconut

1 c. pecan pieces

Preheat oven to 350° F. Combine brownie mix, ¼ c. water, ⅔ c. oil, and 2 eggs (2 T. dry powdered eggs + ¼ c. water). Pour batter into greased 9x13-inch baking pan.

Place butter and cream cheese in small saucepan; cook on medium heat until cream cheese is completely melted and mixture is well blended, stirring frequently. Stir in brown sugar. Add coconut and pecans; mix well. (Mixture will be thick.) Drop spoonfuls of cream cheese mixture over brownie batter in pan.

Bake 30 minutes or until toothpick inserted in center comes out clean. Cool 1 hour. Store leftover brownies in refrigerator.

German Chocolate Brownies

Making Delicious Breakfasts with Powdered Eggs

When I was growing up and my dad had a project for us on a Saturday, he would cook breakfast to get us out of bed. As soon as we finished eating, he would announce, "Well, now that you're all up and fed, I have a little project for you." Now you can entice your family out of bed in the morning with a warm breakfast—and save money, too.

You might be surprised to learn that you can use powdered eggs to make dishes such as French toast, crepes, and German pancakes. Just mix everything together like you would with fresh eggs, but substitute the dry powdered eggs and required water. It's just like baking with powdered eggs—easy!

> 1 medium egg = 1 T. dry powdered eggs + 2 T. water
> 1 large egg = 1½ T. dry powdered eggs + 3 T. water
> 1 extra large egg = 2 T. dry powdered eggs + ¼ C. water

Tips for Making Delicious Breakfasts with Powdered Eggs

1. Just mix the dry powdered eggs and necessary water into your batter.

2. If you're nervous about trying powdered eggs, start by using half fresh eggs and half powdered eggs, then work up to using only powdered eggs.

3. If your recipe calls for mixing eggs and milk together (i.e., French toast), first mix dry powdered eggs and dry powdered milk together before adding the necessary water for both ingredients. This will make it easier for both powders to dissolve in the water.

4. Make it easy! Don't count out more than two tablespoons of either dry powdered eggs or water. Remember, there are 16 tablespoons in one cup, and since I know you don't want to flip back to the tablespoon–cup chart, here it is again.

    > 2 tablespoons = ⅛ cup
    > 4 tablespoons = ¼ cup
    > 6 tablespoons = ⅓ cup

8 tablespoons = ½ cup
10 tablespoons = ⅔ cup
12 tablespoons = ¾ cup

Action Steps

On three separate days, make a different breakfast recipe where you substitute powdered eggs for fresh eggs. You can try some of my favorite recipes or your own. Commit to it today by filling in the recipes and dates below.

The three breakfast recipes I'll make with powdered eggs are:

1._____/Date:_____

2._____/Date:_____

3._____/Date:_____

Blender Crepes, page 98

Favorite Breakfast Recipes Using Powdered Eggs

French Toast Casserole

This is a great way to serve French toast to a group without getting stuck behind a griddle.

2¼ c. whole or evaporated milk (¾ c. +

1½ T. dry powdered milk +

1¼ c. water)

½ c. sugar

1½ t. cinnamon

2 extra large eggs, slightly beaten (¼ c.

dry powdered eggs + ½ c. water)

5½ c. French or other firm bread, in

¾-inch cubes

½ c. pecans, chopped (optional)

maple syrup

Heat oven to 350° F. Mix milk, sugar, cinnamon, and eggs in large bowl with wire whisk until well blended. Stir in bread cubes and pecans. Pour into ungreased 1½-quart casserole. Bake uncovered 40 to 45 minutes or until knife inserted 1 inch from edge of casserole comes out clean. Top each serving with maple sauce (recipe follows). Serves 4.

Maple Sauce

½ c. butter

2 T. water

1 extra large egg (2 T. dry powdered

eggs + ¼ c. water)

1 c. sugar

1 t. maple extract or 2 T. pure maple

syrup

Melt butter in 1-quart saucepan over low heat; do not allow to simmer. Remove from heat. Mix water and egg; stir into butter until blended. Stir in sugar. Cook over medium-low heat, stirring constantly, until sugar is dissolved and mixture begins to boil. Remove from heat and stir in maple extract. Cool at least 10 minutes before serving. Store covered in refrigerator.

German Oven Pancake

This breakfast is so tasty that it could be a dessert!

¼ c. butter or margarine

1½ c. milk (4½ T. dry powdered milk +
    1½ c. water)

¾ c. flour

⅓ c. sugar

3 eggs (3 T. dry powdered eggs + ⅓ c.
    water)

¼ t. salt

3 c. strawberries

2 T. sugar

8 oz. sour cream

¼ c. brown sugar

Preheat oven to 400° F. Place butter in 9-inch pie plate. Bake 5 minutes or until butter is melted. Raise heat to 450° F. Place milk, flour, sugar, eggs, and salt in blender and mix on medium speed until smooth. Remove pie plate from oven and immediately pour in mixture. Return to oven. Bake for 20 minutes at 450° F. Lower heat to 350° F and bake for 8 to 10 minutes more until edges are puffed and browned. (A well will form in middle of pancake.) Toss strawberries with 2 tablespoons sugar. Spoon into center of hot pancake. To serve, cut into wedges. Serve sour cream and brown sugar to top strawberries. (If you don't have fresh fruit, omit sour cream and brown sugar and simply top with syrup.) Serves 4. *Tip: If doubling the recipe, bake in a 9x13-inch pan.*

French Toast with Orange Syrup

This recipe is easy and chock-full of food-storage ingredients.

3 eggs (3 T. dry powdered eggs +
    ⅓ c. water)

1 c. milk (3 T. dry powdered milk +
    1 c. water)

2 T. sugar

¼ t. salt

⅛ t. ground cinnamon

⅛ t. ground nutmeg

8 slices day-old French bread, 1 inch
    thick

In a bowl, beat eggs. Beat in milk, sugar, salt, cinnamon, and nutmeg. Soak slices of bread for 30 seconds on each side. Cook on a hot, greased griddle until golden brown on both sides and cooked through. Serve with warm orange syrup. Serves 4.

Orange Syrup

3 c. fresh orange juice

½ c. sugar

1 t. grated orange peel

2 t. butter

Combine juice, sugar, and orange peel in a medium saucepan over medium-high heat. Bring to a full boil, stirring to dissolve sugar. Reduce heat to a low boil and cook to a thick syrup (liquid will be reduced by half), about 15 minutes. Add the butter and whisk to combine. Cool slightly before serving. *Tip: Begin making the orange syrup before you start the French toast so they are ready at the same time.*

Blender Crepes

Crepes are perfect for using your food storage, since they contain eggs, milk, sugar, flour, and salt. And you blend it all in the blender, so there is no mess!

4 eggs (¼ c. dry powdered eggs + ½ c. water)

1 c. flour

1 c. milk (3 T. dry powdered milk + 1 c. water)

2 t. butter, melted

2 t. sugar

½ t. salt

Measure all ingredients into blender, then mix until smooth. Pour scant ¼ cup batter onto lightly greased 8-inch pan. (Your pan is hot enough when you throw water on it and the water "dances" around.) Tilt pan to coat bottom evenly with batter. Cook over medium heat until brown, then turn to brown other side. Place cream cheese and fresh berries or jam down the center of each crepe, then roll crepe like a burrito and dust with powdered sugar. Serves 4.

Overnight Caramel French Toast

A delectable combination of caramel rolls and French toast.

1 c. brown sugar

½ c. butter

2 T. corn syrup

12 slices white or whole-wheat bread

¼ c. sugar

2 t. ground cinnamon, divided

6 eggs (⅓ c. dry powdered eggs + ⅔ c. water)

1½ c. milk (¼ c. + ½ T. dry powdered milk + 1½ c. water)

1½ t. vanilla extract

In a small saucepan, bring brown sugar, butter, and corn syrup to a boil over medium heat, stirring constantly. Remove from heat. Pour into a greased 9x13-inch baking dish. Top with six slices of bread. Combine sugar and ½ teaspoon cinnamon; sprinkle half over bread. Place remaining bread on top. Sprinkle with remaining cinnamon-sugar; set aside. In a large bowl, beat eggs, milk, vanilla, and remaining cinnamon. Pour over bread. Cover and refrigerate for 8 hours or overnight. Remove from refrigerator 30 minutes before baking. Bake, uncovered, at 350° F for 30 to 35 minutes. Serves 6.

Grandma Kerr's Famous Sourdough Waffles

My sister-in-law introduced this new tradition to our family, and you may want to adopt it for yours!

Step 1: Make Sourdough Starter (at least 12 hours ahead of time)

In a large glass, plastic or ceramic bowl, combine:

> 2 c. white flour
>
> 1 c. milk (3 T. dry powdered milk + 1 c.
>   water)
>
> 1 c. plain yogurt (not vanilla) with
>   active cultures

Mix until smooth with a plastic or wooden spoon or whisk. (Never use a metal bowl or utensil with sourdough, as the metal will leach, ruining the batter and the bowl or utensil.) Cover bowl with a cloth and put it in a warm place. After several hours, starter should be bubbly and produce a pleasant yeasty smell. The longer the starter sits, the better the finished product will taste and smell.

Step 2: Make Waffles

Turn on waffle iron, then stir down sourdough starter and add:

> 2 eggs (2 T. dry egg powder + ¼ c.
>   water)
>
> 2 tablespoons sugar
>
> 1 teaspoon salt
>
> ¼ c. vegetable oil

Mix until completely smooth. When waffle iron is ready, add 1 teaspoon baking soda to batter. Combine thoroughly and use immediately. When waffles are done, top with your favorite syrup, jam, or jelly. These waffles make a great dessert, too. Try them with vanilla ice cream, chocolate syrup, and whipped cream. Bon appétit! *Note: This batter does not keep well, even in the refrigerator. If you have leftover batter, make up the waffles and freeze the finished product, or invite some friends to come join in the feast.*

Extending Fresh Eggs Using Powdered Eggs

Obviously, you can't always substitute powdered eggs for fresh eggs, since things like boiled eggs and poached eggs must be made from fresh, intact eggs. However, you can use powdered eggs to extend your expensive fresh eggs in scrambled eggs, egg bakes, and omelets. Egg breakfasts are quick, filling, and high in protein, so it's very worthwhile to learn how to make them cheaper or in a pinch. The egg measurements are still the same:

> 1 medium egg = 1 T. dry powdered eggs + 2 T. water
>
> 1 large egg = 1 ½ T. dry powdered eggs + 3 T. water
>
> 1 extra large egg = 2 T. dry powdered eggs + ¼ c. water

Tip: Since most baking recipes call for two eggs, buy a 2-tablespoon or ⅛-cup measuring cup (also called a coffee scoop), and store it in your can of powdered eggs.

Tips for Using Powdered Eggs in Your Recipes

1. Use powdered eggs in any egg-based breakfast recipe that doesn't contain boiled, poached, or fried eggs. If you're nervous about how it will turn out, start by using one-quarter powdered eggs and three-quarters fresh eggs. Then work up to using all powdered eggs.

2. Remember that it's okay if you or your family doesn't like an egg-based breakfast with all powdered eggs. Just experiment until you discover the mix of powdered eggs and fresh eggs that your family does like. Even if you use the equivalent of one powdered egg instead of one fresh egg in the recipe, you are still saving money.

Don't Just Take My Word for It

Here are some of the comments I've received about powdered eggs on my website.

"Using the powdered eggs was so easy. You're right—we couldn't tell a difference! I made some scrambled eggs with them—I included dried onion, red pepper flakes, and some cheese at the end. They were quite good!"–Hannah J.

"We broke open our first can of powdered eggs on Friday for breakfast. My 4 kids ate the equivalent of 20 eggs (scrambled)! Who would have thought?"–Jean Marie D.

Action Steps

On three separate days, try an egg-based breakfast recipe where you substitute powdered eggs for fresh eggs. You can try some of my favorite recipes or your own. Commit to it by filling in the recipes and dates below.

The three egg-based breakfast recipes I'll make with powdered eggs are:

1._____/Date:_____

2._____/Date:_____

3._____/Date:_____

Baked Denver Omelet, page 102

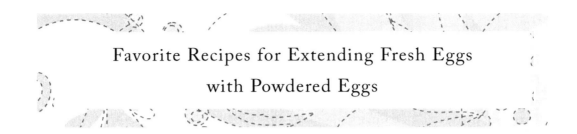

Favorite Recipes for Extending Fresh Eggs with Powdered Eggs

Breakfast Casserole

This delicious casserole is hearty and filling.

6 oz. pork sausage

½ c. bell pepper, chopped

1 can (4.5 oz.) green chiles

1 pkg. (20 oz.) hash browns

2 c. shredded cheddar cheese

4 extra large eggs (½ c. dry powdered
     eggs + 1 c. water)

1 c. milk (3 T. dry powdered milk +1 c.
     water)

1 medium tomato, chopped

Heat oven to 350° F. Spray an 8-inch square baking dish with nonstick spray. In a large skillet, cook the sausage, bell pepper, and chiles until the sausage is browned. Drain. Layer half of the potatoes, half the sausage mixture, and ¾ cup cheese. Repeat. Combine eggs and milk in a bowl, and beat well. Pour evenly over the potato, sausage, and cheese mixture and press lightly to make sure the egg mixture is distributed evenly. Cover with foil and bake for 35 minutes. Uncover and add tomato and remaining ½ cup cheese. Bake uncovered for an additional 10 to 15 minutes or until a knife inserted in center comes out clean. Let stand 5 minutes before serving.

Baked Denver Omelet

I serve this omelet with fruit and homemade bread, and it's always a hit.

8 eggs (½ c. dry powdered eggs + 1 c.
     water)

½ c. whole or evaporated milk (3 T. dry
     powdered milk + ½ c. water)

1 c. shredded cheddar cheese

1 c. finely chopped fully cooked ham

¼ c. finely chopped green pepper

¼ c. finely chopped green or white
onion

In a bowl, whisk eggs and milk together. Stir in cheese, ham, green pepper, and onion. Pour into a greased 8x8-inch square baking dish. Bake at 400° F for 25 minutes or until golden brown. Serves 4. Variation: Add a 4 oz. can of green chiles before baking.

Ham Breakfast Quiche

This is a great dish to serve at a brunch.

6 slices white bread

2 c. diced ham

1 green pepper, diced

½ onion, diced

4 c. shredded cheddar cheese

4 extra large eggs (½ c. dry powdered
eggs + 1 c. water)

3 c. milk (½ c. + 1 T. dry powdered milk
+ 3 c. water)

3 T. butter

4 T. flour

Cut crusts off bread. Butter bread and put buttered side down in a 9x13-inch baking dish. Sauté green pepper and onion in butter.

Mix flour with shredded cheese. Beat eggs and milk together. Mix together ham, green pepper, onion, and cheese mixed with flour. Pour over bread. Bake uncovered at 375° F for 50 to 60 minutes. *Tip: You can put the quiche together and refrigerate it uncooked for up to 24 hours, then place in oven and bake.*

Breakfast Burritos

If your family hasn't yet tried scrambled powdered eggs, this is the perfect recipe.

4 burrito-size tortillas

8 extra large eggs (¾ c. dry powdered
eggs + 1½ c. water)

½ c. cheese

salsa

Scramble eggs. (If you're using egg powder, mix the powder and water together and add to hot frying pan, then scramble as you would fresh eggs.) Sprinkle cheese on tortillas and heat slightly in microwave. Add eggs and salsa to taste. Wrap like a burrito by folding in the two ends and rolling until closed. Serves 4. *Variation: Add cooked breakfast sausage to the eggs, and use fruit salsa instead of regular salsa.*

Blender Baked Egg Roll

This recipe has gourmet flare without the mess!

6 eggs (⅓ c. dry powdered eggs + ⅔ c.
    water)
1 c. milk (3 T. powdered milk + 1 c.
    water)
½ c. all purpose flour
½ t. salt
¼ t. pepper
1 c. shredded cheddar or pepper Jack
    cheese

Place eggs and milk in blender. Add flour, salt, and pepper; cover and process until smooth. Pour into a greased 9x13-inch pan. Bake at 450° F for 20 minutes or until eggs are set. Sprinkle with cheese. Roll up in pan, starting with short side. Place with seam side down on a serving platter. Cut into ¾-inch slices. Serves 6. *Tip: If it puffs up, just poke holes in the "bubbles" and it will still roll up fine.*

Ultimate Egg Croissant

A delicious sandwich for any occasion.

2 medium croissants, split, lightly
    toasted
2 T. cream cheese
2 extra large eggs (1/4 c. dry egg
    powder + ½ c. water)
2 T. chives
1 t. onion powder
1/8 t. pepper
6 slices bacon

Scramble eggs. (If you're using egg powder, mix powder and water together and add to hot frying pan, then scramble as you would fresh eggs.) Stir chives and onion powder into cream cheese. Spread thin layer of cream cheese on lightly toasted croissants; top with eggs and bacon. Serve warm.

Egg Sandwich

Try these when you don't have time to sit down for breakfast.

4 English muffins, toasted
4 slices cheese (your choice)
8 extra large eggs (¾ c. dry powdered
    eggs + 1½ c. water)

Scramble eggs. (If using egg powder, mix powder and water together and add to hot frying pan, then scramble as you would fresh eggs.) Place one slice of cheese on each of four English muffin halves, then place warm eggs on top to melt cheese. Top with remaining muffin halves.

STEP 6

USING WHOLE WHEAT

Whole-Wheat EZ Bread, page 127

STEP 6

USING WHOLE WHEAT

The Whole Truth about Wheat

You're already cooking with powdered milk and powdered eggs. Now it's time to cook with whole wheat. First we'll cook with the whole wheat grain, then move on to cracking wheat and cooking with it. When we've mastered that, we'll start disguising whole-wheat flour in baking. Finally, we'll make delicious whole-wheat bread that's better than what you can buy in the store—for a fraction of the cost.

Make sure you don't stop using powdered milk and powdered eggs in your recipes. I've made it easy to keep substituting, because my whole-wheat recipes also contain powdered milk and powdered eggs.

Using Wheat Berries

The terms *wheat grain*, *wheat berry*, and *wheat kernel* all refer to the same thing—the entire wheat grain that you get when you buy wheat. When cooked whole, they are simply delicious, and you can eat them as a cereal, toss them into salads for extra nutrition, or even use them to make a mock pasta salad.

How to Cook Whole Wheat Berries

Thermos Method

1 c. wheat
2 c. boiling water
½ t. salt

Pick over wheat berries for any foreign bits, then rinse. Place ingredients in one-quart thermos. Screw top on loosely. Leave overnight.

Stovetop Method

1 c. wheat
2 c. boiling water
½ t. salt

Pick over wheat berries for any foreign bits, then rinse. Place ingredients in a saucepan and bring to a boil. Reduce heat and simmer for 1 hour or more tender. Drain and cool.

Slow Cooker Method

1 c. wheat
2½ cups water
½ teaspoon salt

Pick over wheat berries for any foreign bits, then rinse. Place ingredients in slow cooker. Cook 6 to 8 hours or overnight on LOW. Makes 4 to 6 servings.

> *Tip: Cooked wheat may be stored in an airtight container in the refrigerator for up to two weeks. To freeze cooked wheat, spread it in a thin layer on a cookie sheet and place it in the freezer overnight. Then divide the wheat into small freezer bags and place them in the freezer so that you can thaw out only the amount of wheat you need.*

Tips for Using Cooked Whole Wheat Kernels or Berries

1. Have a great breakfast waiting in the morning by cooking wheat berries in your slow cooker overnight. Add dried fruit, spices, and sweetener as you would with oatmeal. You can even serve the "cereal" with milk.

2. Out of pasta? Substitute wheat berries for pasta in your favorite pasta salad. The salad will be far more nutritious, and you'll save money.

3. Top your favorite tossed salad with nutritious wheat berries.

4. Add wheat berries to your favorite soup for extra nutrition or as substitute for rice or barley.

Action Steps

Try using wheat berries three separate times. You can try some of my favorite recipes or your own. Commit to it by filling in the recipes and dates below.

The three recipes in which I'll use whole wheat berries are:

1._____/Date:_____

2._____/Date:_____

3._____/Date:_____

Blender Wheat Pancakes, page 112

Favorite Recipes Using Wheat Berries

Feta Wheat Berry Salad

This wonderful recipe was sent to me by Charlene, one of my website friends. You could add some grilled chicken and call it dinner!

1 c. whole wheat berries

½ c. feta cheese, diced (I like the basil-
and-sundried-tomato variety)

½ c. red onion, minced

½ c. cucumber, peeled, seeded, and
chopped

¼ c. julienne strips of bottled red
peppers, drained and chopped

¼ c. pepperoncini salad peppers,
chopped

¼ c. mixed fresh herbs (parsley, mint,
thyme, and basil), minced, plus extra

for garnish

1 T. kalamata black olives, pitted,
brine-cured, chopped

1 garlic clove, minced

5 T. olive oil

2 T. fresh lemon juice

1 T. balsamic vinegar

Pick over wheat berries and remove any foreign bits, then rinse. Add wheat berries to boiling salted water and reduce to a simmer. Cook the wheat for 1 hour or until tender. Drain and cool.

Stir together the wheat berries, cheese, onion, cucumber, roasted pepper, olives, pepperoncini, herbs, and garlic. In a separate bowl, mix the olive oil, lemon juice, and vinegar. Mix everything together. Garnish with herbs. Variation: Use 1 diced avocado, 2 diced Roma tomatoes, 1 cup sliced artichoke hearts, and regular olives.

Roasted Wheat Kernels

A fun alternative to popcorn and just as delicious.

¼ c. wheat berries

½ T. oil

⅛ t. salt

Heat a small amount of oil in a skillet. Add wheat berries and cook until they pop. (They don't expand as much as popcorn does.) Swirl kernels around in the pan to prevent burning. Sprinkle with salt while hot. Yield: about ⅓ cup.

Wheat Berry Salad with Apples and Cashews

Another delicious recipe from Charlene.

1 c. whole wheat berries

5 c. water

3 T. vegetable oil

½ c. orange juice

2 T. red wine vinegar

2 t. ground coriander

½ t. ground cinnamon

2 Granny Smith apples, cored, diced

2 T. fresh mint, finely chopped

½ c. cashews, toasted, coarsely chopped

1 green onion, minced

1 c. dried, sweetened cranberries

feta cheese (optional)

Pick over the wheat berries for any foreign bits, then rinse. Bring wheat berries to a boil, reduce heat, and simmer for 1 hour or more until tender. Drain and cool. In a small bowl, mix vegetable oil, orange juice, vinegar, coriander, and cinnamon. Set aside.

To wheat berries, add apples, mint, shallots, and cranberries. Toss with dressing to coat. Prior to serving, add roasted cashews. *Tip: If you make this salad ahead of time, you will need to add more dressing before serving, as some of the ingredients will absorb the liquid.*

Gourmet Banana Nut Cookies

These cookies have a moist consistency similar to that of pumpkin cookies.

⅔ c. brown sugar

⅓ c. white sugar

⅔ c. shortening

2 eggs (2 T. dry powdered eggs + ¼ c. water)

1 t. vanilla

1 c. mashed bananas plus ¼ c. water

¾ c. whole wheat berries

2 c. flour

2 t. baking powder

¼ t. salt

¼ t. baking soda

¾ c. (6 oz.) chocolate chips

¾ c. chopped walnuts, optional

Beat together sugar and shortening until fluffy. Add eggs and beat well, then add vanilla. In a blender, blend wheat berries, water, and mashed bananas for 4 to 5 minutes. To egg mixture, add banana mixture alternately with mixture of flour, baking powder, salt, and soda; mix well. Stir in chocolate chips and walnuts. Refrigerate for 1 to 2 hours. Drop by rounded teaspoons onto lightly greased baking sheets. Bake at 350° F degrees for about 10 minutes. Cool on rack. If desired, top with frosting. Yield: 4 to 5 dozen cookies.

Frosting

½ c. butter or margarine, softened

4 c. powdered sugar

dash of salt

approx. ¼ c. milk (¾ T. dry powdered
       milk and ¼ c. water)

1 t. vanilla

Beat butter, sugar, and salt until thoroughly blended. Add milk and vanilla. Add more milk as needed.

Blender Wheat Pancakes

The simplest, easiest to clean up, and most delicious whole-grain pancakes you will ever make.

1 c. milk (3 T. dry powdered milk + 1 c.
       water)

1 c. wheat kernels, whole & uncooked

2 eggs (2 T. dry powdered eggs + ¼ c.
       water)

2 t. baking powder

1 ½ t. salt

2 T. oil

2 T. honey or sugar

Put milk and wheat kernels in blender. Blend on highest speed for 4 or 5 minutes or until batter is smooth. Add eggs, oil, baking powder, salt, and honey or sugar. Blend on LOW. For each pancake, pour some batter from blender onto a hot, greased griddle or into a large frying pan. Cook, flipping pancake when bubbles pop and create holes.

Tip: Visit www.everydayfoodstorage. net/videos to watch a video demonstrating how to make blender wheat pancakes.

Blender Wheat Waffles

These whole-grain waffles are so divine that you'll never use waffle mix again.

1 c. milk (3 T. dry powdered milk + 1 c. water)

1 c. + 1 T. wheat kernels, whole and uncooked

2 eggs (2 T. dry powdered eggs + ¼ c. water)

2 t. baking powder

½ t. salt

¼ cup oil

2 T. sugar

Put milk and wheat kernels in blender. Blend on highest speed for 4 or 5 minutes or until batter is smooth. Add eggs, oil, baking powder, salt, and honey or sugar. Blend on LOW. From the blender jar, pour batter into hot, prepared waffle iron, then close waffle iron to cook. Check waffle often. (These waffles take slightly longer to cook than regular waffles.)

Variation: Banana Blender Wheat Waffles

Increase wheat to 1 cup plus 2 tablespoons. Mash two ripe bananas and blend them into batter before pouring into waffle iron. If desired, sprinkle chopped walnuts on batter before closing waffle iron. Prepare and cook as directed above. Serve with Hot Caramel Sauce (below).

Hot Caramel Sauce

½ c. buttermilk (1½ T. dry powdered milk + ½ c. water + ½ T. vinegar or lemon juice)

2 cups sugar

½ cup butter

2 T. corn syrup

2 t. baking soda

1 t. vanilla

Mix ingredients except vanilla in a large pot and boil for 3 minutes. Sauce will turn a caramel color towards the end of boiling. Add vanilla after removing from heat.

Wheat Berry Salad with Apples and Cashews, page 111

Using Cracked Wheat

In most recipes, cracked wheat can be used instead of rice or nuts. In fact, many recipes actually *taste* better when you substitute cracked wheat for rice or nuts. Cracked wheat can also be used as a meat extender or meat substitute, and either way it will save you money, cut the dish's fat content, and vamp up the dish's fiber content. Try all these options—you just might love them all.

Cracking the Whole Wheat Berry

You can crack dry wheat in small amounts (¼ cup at a time) in your blender using the PULSE option, or you can use a coffee grinder. Coffee grinders are inexpensive and make cracking wheat so much easier, but before you purchase one, use your blender until you know how often you'll use cracked wheat.

> *Tip: For a video that shows how to crack wheat in the blender, visit www.everydayfoodstorage.net/videos.*

Cooking Cracked Wheat

Cooking cracked wheat is just as simple as cooking white rice. In fact it's as easy as 1–2–3: 1 cup of wheat plus 2 cups of water makes 3 cups of cooked wheat. Bring cracked wheat, water, and ½ teaspoon salt to a boil. Cover and cook on low heat for 10 to 20 minutes or until tender.

Tips for Using Cooked Cracked Wheat

1. To use whole wheat as a meat extender, pick a sauce recipe (like sloppy-joe sauce or spaghetti sauce) that contains ground meat. Just add ½ cup cooked cracked wheat for every pound of ground meat.

2. Out of rice? Use cooked cracked wheat instead.

3. Use cracked wheat as a quick hot cereal in the morning. Cook ¼ cup cracked

wheat with ½ cup water in the microwave for 3 to 5 minutes or until tender.

4. Substitute cracked wheat for nuts in gelatin or green salads.

Action Steps

Try using cracked wheat three different ways. You can try it in some of my favorite recipes or your own. Commit to it by filling in the recipes and dates below.

The three recipes I'll make with cracked wheat are:

1._____/Date:_____

2._____/Date:_____

3._____/Date:_____

Strawberry "Nut" Molded Salad, page 116

Favorite Recipes Using Cracked Wheat

Strawberry "Nut" Molded Salad

The cracked wheat in this gelatin salad gives it a wonderful texture. Your family will love it, and no one will guess there's wheat in it!

1 small pkg. strawberry or raspberry
   gelatin

1 c. boiling water

1 c. cooked cracked wheat

1 c. whipped topping

½ c. sugar

2 c. mashed fresh strawberries

Combine gelatin and water, then refrigerate until syrupy and add the remaining ingredients. (Because the mixture goes from syrupy to gel very quickly, check it 15 to 20 minutes after you put it in the refrigerator, and every 2 minutes thereafter.) Refrigerate until firm (several hours or overnight), then slice. Serve each slice on a bed of lettuce with a dollop of whipped cream or whipped topping, sprinkled with cooked cracked wheat.

Cracked Wheat Sausage

This is great when you feel like eating sausage but don't want all the fat.

1 c. cooked cracked wheat

1½ t. sage

2–3 dashes onion salt

2–3 dashes garlic salt

1 t. beef flavor base

1 t. Worcestershire sauce

1 extra large egg (2 T. dry powdered
   eggs + ¼ c. water)

1 T. brown sugar

dash cayenne pepper

3–4 drops of liquid smoke

1 T. flour (if too thin)

Combine all ingredients. Form into ½-inch-thick patties. Fry in small amount of oil.

Cowboy Chocolate-Chip Cookies

This version of everyone's favorite cookie uses cracked wheat as a nut substitute.

Beat together:

1 c. shortening

2 eggs (2 T. dry powdered eggs + ¼ c. water)

¾ c. brown sugar

¾ c. white sugar

1 t. vanilla

Add and beat:

2 c. flour

½ t. baking soda

1 c. cracked wheat, cooked

Stir in:

1 c. chocolate chips

Drop by rounded teaspoonfuls on ungreased cookie sheet. Bake at 325˚ F for about 8 to 10 minutes or until light golden brown

Cracked-Wheat Meat Loaf

This meat loaf is so delicious that no one will guess it's got more fiber (and less fat!) than regular meat loaf.

2½ c. cooked cracked wheat

2 lbs. ground beef

1¼ c. milk (3¾ T. dry powdered milk + 1¼ c. water)

¼ t. pepper

2 t. salt

¼ c. ketchup

1 extra large egg (2 T. dry powdered eggs + ¼ c. water)

1 T. Worcestershire sauce

1 t. dry mustard

1 envelope onion soup mix

Mix all ingredients together. Turn into greased loaf pan or shallow baking dish.

If desired, spread surface with a thin layer of ketchup. Bake at 325˚ F for 1 hour.

Beef Tacos

This is a great way to extend your ground beef.

1 lb. ground beef

1 pkg. taco seasoning mix

¾ c. water

1 c. cooked cracked wheat

12 taco shells

assorted toppings such as shredded
    lettuce, chopped tomato, and
    shredded cheese

Brown meat in large skillet on medium-high heat. Drain fat. Stir in seasoning mix, cooked cracked wheat, and water. Bring to boil. Reduce heat to low; simmer 5 minutes, stirring occasionally. Spoon into warmed taco shells. Serve with assorted toppings.

Tomato Cracked-Wheat Pilaf

This savory, easy-to-prepare dish has an international feel.

¼ c. butter

1 c. uncooked coarsely cracked wheat,
    sifted to remove any flour

2½ c. chicken broth

¼ c. chopped green onion

¼ c. minced fresh parsley

¼ c. chopped tomato

Simmer dry cracked wheat in butter until thoroughly coated and bubbly. Fry onion separately until soft and yellow. Mix together and stir in chicken broth, green onions, and parsley. Stir well, and place in a covered 3-quart casserole dish. Bake at 350° F for 10 to 15 minutes. Stir gently with fork and add tomatoes. Bake an additional 10 minutes more or until liquid is absorbed. Fluff with fork and serve warm.

Beef Tacos

Disguising 100% Whole-Wheat Flour in Baking

With hard white wheat available for storage, it's easy to make delicious food with 100% whole-wheat flour. So now that you've got a wheat grinder and can make fresh wheat flour, just follow the steps below. You'll be amazed as you watch your family enjoy eating their favorite recipes made with whole wheat.

Tips for Using Whole-Wheat Flour in Your Recipes

1. Try it in desserts first—who can turn down a cookie?
2. Try using half white flour and half whole-wheat flour. It's not necessary to substitute whole-wheat flour for ALL of the white flour in every recipe, and if you're just starting to use whole-wheat flour, such a shock could turn your family off to wheat. If your family is extra finicky, start with 1 tablespoon of whole-wheat flour in the bottom of each cup of all-purpose flour and increase the amount of whole-wheat flour each time you cook. The important thing is that you're using your wheat flour and increasing nutrient intake where you can.
2. Use recipes that your family already enjoys and is familiar with.
3. Disguise wheat flour—which is light brown in color—in bread, cakes, and cookie recipes that contain brown sugar, molasses, chocolate, or fruit or vegetables (such as bananas, applesauce, zucchini, or carrots).
4. Use whole-wheat flour in recipes that also call for oats or oat flour. Oats have a hearty flavor that helps disguise the flavor of whole wheat.
5. Remember: Don't warn your family that there is whole wheat in the food they're about to eat. If you don't say anything, they'll assume you followed the recipe just as you always have. So sit back and smile to yourself and watch your family members gobble up the food . . . wheat and all!

Don't Just Take My Word for It

Here are some of the comments I've received about whole wheat on my website.

"I made brown sugar zucchini bread [with whole-wheat flour] and thought it was great! I was worried, though, that my kids would be able to tell I'd used whole-wheat flour. But nope, they ate it all and begged for more. Thanks so much for the [tips]!"—Meredith

"I made wheat pancakes this week and loved them."—Stacia

"I made whole-wheat chocolate chip cookies for my kids. I thought for sure they'd be able to tell they looked a little darker . . . but nobody said a thing and they ate them all!" –Keri

Action Steps

On three separate days, try a different recipe where you use whole-wheat flour. Try it in your family's favorite cookie recipe first, or get some inspiration from some of my favorite recipes. Commit to it by filling in the recipes and dates below.

The three recipes I'll make with whole-wheat flour are:

1._____/Date:_____

2._____/Date:_____

3._____/Date:_____

Snickerdoodles, page 122

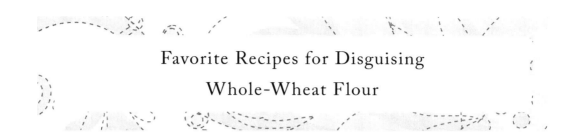

Favorite Recipes for Disguising Whole-Wheat Flour

Oatmeal Cranberry White-Chocolate-Chunk Cookies

These wonderful cookies are perfectly crisp on the outside and chewy on the inside.

⅔ c. butter or margarine, softened

⅔ c. brown sugar

2 extra large eggs (¼ c. dry powdered
    eggs + ¼ c. water)

1½ c. instant oats

1½ c. whole-wheat flour

1 t. baking soda

½ t. salt

6-oz. package dried, sweetened
    cranberries

⅔ c. white chocolate chunks or chips

Preheat oven to 375° F. Using an electric mixer, beat butter or margarine and sugar together in a medium mixing bowl until light and fluffy. Add eggs, mixing well. Combine oats, flour, baking soda, and salt in a separate mixing bowl. Add to butter mixture in several additions, mixing well after each. Stir in sweetened dried cranberries and white chocolate chunks. Drop by rounded teaspoonfuls onto ungreased cookie sheets. Bake for 10 to 12 minutes or until golden brown. Cool on wire rack. Yield: Approx. 2½ dozen cookies.

Whole-Wheat Chocolate-Chip Brownies

These brownies are divine, and chocolate's strong flavor hides the taste of the whole wheat.

2 c. whole-wheat flour

½ t. baking soda

¾ c. oil

121

1 c. brown sugar

2 eggs (2 T. dry powdered eggs + ¼ c.
    water)

½ t. salt

½ c. white sugar

1 t. vanilla

¾ c. walnuts (optional)

¾ c. chocolate chips

Mix all ingredients together except chocolate chips. Grease a 9x13-inch pan, pat the mixture into pan, and sprinkle top with chocolate chips. Bake in a 350° F oven for 20 to 25 minutes.

Snickerdoodles

This is a family favorite that happens to be a great food-storage cookie—even if you decide not to sneak in some whole-wheat flour.

1 c. shortening

1½ c. sugar

2 eggs (2 T. dry powdered eggs + ¼ c.
    water)

2¾ c. flour (I use half whole-wheat
    flour and half all-purpose flour)

2 t. cream of tartar

1 t. soda

¼ t. salt

2 T. sugar

2 t. cinnamon

Preheat oven to 400° F. Mix shortening, 1½ cup sugar, and eggs thoroughly. Blend flour, cream of tartar, soda, and salt; add to wet mixture, blending dough thoroughly. Shape dough in 1-inch balls. Roll in cinnamon-sugar mixture. Place dough balls 2 inches apart on an ungreased baking sheet. Bake 8 to 10 minutes. These cookies puff up at first, then flatten out. Yield: approx. 3 dozen cookies.

Whole-Wheat Pumpkin Bread

For an easy breakfast on the go, just spread a slice of this delicious bread with soft cream cheese.

1 c. canned pumpkin

1 c. white sugar

½ c. brown sugar

2 eggs (2 T. dry powdered eggs + ¼ c.
    water)

½ cup milk (1½ T. dry powdered milk +
    ½ c. water)

¼ c. vegetable oil

2 c. whole-wheat flour

2½ t. baking powder

2 t. pumpkin pie spice

¼ t. salt

Preheat oven to 350° F. Grease a nonstick 9x5-inch loaf pan; set aside. Mix pumpkin, 1 cup sugar, brown sugar, egg whites, milk, and oil in large bowl. Add flour, baking powder, pie spice, and salt; stir just until moistened. Spoon the pumpkin batter into prepared pan. Bake 1 hour or until wooden toothpick inserted in center comes out clean. Run knife or thin spatula around edges of pan to loosen bread; cool in pan on wire rack for 10 minutes. Remove bread from pan to wire rack; cool completely.

Chocolate-Chip Oatmeal Cookies

This is my husband's favorite cookie, and the first time I substituted whole-wheat flour for white flour, he didn't even notice!

Mix until creamy:

  1 c. shortening

  ¾ c. sugar

  ¾ c. brown sugar

  1 t. vanilla

  ½ t. water

Add:

  2 eggs (2 T. dry powdered eggs + ¼ c.
    water)

  2½ c. whole-wheat flour*

  1 t. baking soda

  1 t. salt

  ¾ c. oatmeal

  12 oz. chocolate chips

Bake at 375° F for 10 to 12 minutes. Remove from oven while still light brown in color. Yield: approx. 3 dozen cookies. *When doubling this recipe, try using 4 cups flour and 1½ to 2 cups oatmeal.

Whole-Wheat Pumpkin Bread, page 122

Making Delicious Homemade Bread

If you've eaten homemade bread or bread from a bread machine, you know that it can be dry and have a hard crust that is difficult to cut through. But homemade bread can be the most delicious bread you've ever eaten if it is done right. Homemade bread is definitely more nutritious and much less expensive than the equivalent at a grocery store. If you don't have a bread machine, check your local second-hand store.

Tips for Making Delicious Homemade Whole-Wheat Bread Using Your Recipes

1. Use white wheat (its taste is more subtle), and always use the wheat setting on your bread machine (bread made with whole-wheat flour needs to rise longer than bread made with all-purpose white flour).

2. Add potato flakes to your bread to achieve the soft texture of store-bought bread. (I add ½ cup to mine.) This trick has been used since pioneer days when women would use the cooking water from potatoes in their bread to make it soft. Potato flakes deposit sticky starch into the bubbles that form in baking bread, keeping the air from escaping. And the good news is that Church canneries now carry potato flakes.

3. Place hot bread in a sealed plastic bag or towel to cool. The crust will be much softer, and the bread won't get moldy or dry out as quickly. Plus, a softer crust makes the bread much easier to cut.

4. Experiment with gluten. A good rule of thumb is to use 1 tablespoon of gluten for every cup of whole wheat flour in your recipe. Gluten strengthens the bubbles that form while bread is baking, preventing them from popping too early. This helps ensure that the bread won't sink in the middle. Also, gluten is a form of protein, so adding it to your bread makes the bread even more nutritious. (If you live at an altitude over 3500 feet and use a bread machine and decide to add gluten to your bread, decreasethe yeast by half to avoid getting a misshapen loaf of bread.)

5. Create your own dough enhancer by adding gluten (see #4) and white vinegar. (Use the same amount of vinegar as yeast.)

6. If you're not using a bread machine, roll the dough into a 8x12-inch rectangle. Beginning with the short side, loosely roll the dough, just as you would when making cinnamon rolls. Pinch edges and place in a greased bread pan to rise. (Rolling the dough out will keep the air bubbles in the bread more uniform and will give the bread a better texture.)

7. When using a bread machine at altitudes over 3500 feet, use less yeast. Bread dough rises faster at higher altitudes, and since the bread machine uses a timed process, it won't start baking the bread soon enough. I live at high altitude, and I use only half the yeast called for in my bread recipes.

8. Simplify the process by making bread-mix bags. Fill zip-top bags with all the dry ingredients in your bread recipe (minus the yeast), and place them in your refrigerator. Now you can always have fresh homemade bread ready and waiting—with no mess!

Action Steps

Make bread or rolls three separate times, substituting whole-wheat flour for at least part of the white flour. You can use your own bread or roll recipes or try some of my favorites. Commit to it by filling in the recipes and dates below.

The three bread or roll recipes I'll make with whole-wheat flour are:

1._____/Date:_____

2._____/Date:_____

3._____/Date:_____

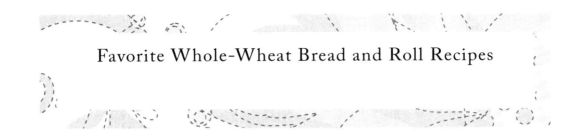

Favorite Whole-Wheat Bread and Roll Recipes

Lorraine's Whole-Wheat Cinnamon Rolls

These rolls are so light and fluffy that you'd never guess they're made with whole wheat.

Dough

    2½ c. warm water

    2 T. yeast

    ½ c. sugar

    3 extra large eggs (⅓ c. dry powdered
        eggs + ⅔ c. water)

    1 t. salt

    6 T. oil or butter, melted

    ½ c. potato flakes

    1 T. gluten

    7 c. flour (4 c. whole-wheat flour and
        3 c. all-purpose flour)

Filling

    ⅓ c. butter, softened

    ⅔ c. sugar

    ⅓ c. brown sugar

    2 T. cinnamon

In a large mixing bowl, dissolve yeast in warm water. Add sugar, eggs, salt, oil or butter, potato flakes, and gluten. With mixer on medium speed beat for 2 to 3 minutes or until smooth. Stir in enough flour to form a soft dough.

Turn onto a floured surface; knead until smooth and elastic. Divide dough into two pieces. With a rolling pin on a floured surface, roll each piece into a 8x12-inch rectangle that is ¼ inch thick.

Spread each rectangle with soft butter, then sprinkle liberally with sugar and cinnamon. Sprinkle with raisins, if desired. Roll up jelly-roll style, starting with a long side; pinch seam to seal. Cut 1-inch-thick rolls with dental floss or sharp serrated knife. Place in greased 9x13-inch or two 8x8-inch pans.

Let rolls rise until double in size. Bake at 350° F for about 20 minutes. Frost with cream cheese frosting. Yield: 18 rolls.

Best-Ever Cream Cheese Frosting

½ c. (1 stick) unsalted butter, softened

4 oz. cream cheese, softened

2 c. powdered sugar (confectioners' sugar)

1 t. vanilla extract

Cream butter, cheese, and vanilla together: Gradually add powdereed sugar, stirring until smooth.

Best Whole-Wheat Bread Recipe for Bread Machines

This recipe always produces a great loaf of bread.

1 ⅔ c. water

2 T. butter, softened

⅓ c. brown sugar

2 t. salt

4⅔ c. whole-wheat flour

1 T. wheat gluten (I use Vital® brand)

⅓ c. potato flakes

3 t. yeast*

3 t. white vinegar*

In order listed, place ingredients, except yeast in bread machine. Create a small well in the middle of the dry ingredients and place yeast in the formed well. Set bread machine. Yield: 2-pound loaf. *High altitude: Decrease yeast and vinegar to 1½ teaspoons each.

Whole-Wheat EZ Bread

This bread tastes just like store bought!

1¼ c. warm water

1 T. yeast*

1 T. white vinegar*

¼ c. honey or ⅓ c. sugar

2¾ c. whole-wheat flour

¼ c. wheat gluten

1 t. salt

2 T. dry powdered milk

1 T. butter/oil

¼ c. potato flakes

Mix ingredients in order listed for 12 to 15 minutes in mixer bowl with dough hook attachment. Let rise until double—1 to 1½ hours. Punch dough down, then shape into loaf or rolls. Let rise again until double and bake at 375° F for 20 to 30 minutes until crust is golden brown and bread sounds hollow when lightly tapped. *High altitude: Decrease yeast and vinegar to ½ tablespoon each. *Tip: If making this bread in a bread machine, follow the machine's directions for wheat or whole-grain bread and add the ingredients in the recommended order.*

> *Tip: Visit www.everydayfoodstorage. net/videos to watch a video demonstrating how to make whole wheat bread.*

Sandwich Pockets

While these pockets taste great with any kind of sandwich filling, they are perfect for messy fillings like tuna salad, egg salad, and chicken salad.

    1 c. lukewarm water

    2 T. olive oil or canola oil

    1 t. sugar

    ½ t. salt

    3 c. flour (I use either whole-wheat flour or half all-purpose and half whole-wheat)

    1½ t. yeast

Dough by Hand:

Dissolve yeast in warm water. Add oil, sugar, and salt. Slowly mix in flour and knead. Cover and let rise for 45 minutes.

Dough in Bread Machine:

Add ingredients in the order specified by the user's manual for your bread machine. You don't want your dough to rise for more than one hour. Most bread machine dough cycles will "beat" down the dough, and you'll want to take the dough out before it does that. Consult your user's manual for timing and instructions.

Preheat oven to 375° F. When dough is ready, separate it into 6 equal portions. Using a rolling pin, roll out dough to ⅛-inch-thick circles. Let dough rest for 5 minutes. Put ¼ to ½ cup of filling on each circle. Fold dough in half over the filling and clamp edges with fork for a secure closure. Brush the tops with an egg-white wash (1 egg white beaten with 1 to 2 T. water) if you want them to look professional. Bake for 15 to 20 minutes.

Dilly Bread

This bread is so satisfying that it feels like a meal.

    2¼ t. yeast

    ¼ c. warm water

    1 c. cottage cheese

    1 egg (1½ T. dry egg powder + 3 T. water)

2 T. sugar

1 T. onion, minced

2 t. dill seed

1 t. salt

¼ t. baking soda

1 T. butter, softened

2¼–2½ c. flour

Soften yeast in warm water. Let stand 10 minutes. Heat cottage cheese to lukewarm. In large bowl combine dissolved yeast, egg, sugar, onion, dill seed, salt, and baking soda. Stir in warmed cottage cheese and 1 T. softened butter. Mix thoroughly. Add flour in fourths, beating well after each addition. Cover dough and let rise until double (about 1 hour). Punch down. Turn into greased 2-quart round casserole or 2 loaf pans. Let rise again until doubled. Bake at 350° F for 35 to 40 minutes. Brush with butter and sprinkle with salt.

Bannock

Ideal for when you're in a hurry—and tasty, too!

3 c. flour (any combination of whole-
     wheat and all-purpose)

2 T. baking powder

¼ c. oil

1½ c. water

pinch salt

Preheat oven to 400° F. In a large bowl or mixer, mix ingredients together. Knead with bread hook in mixer for 6 minutes, or knead on a lightly floured surface for about 10 minutes. Let dough rest for 1 minute, then spread it onto a cookie sheet until dough is 1 inch thick. Poke holes in dough using a fork. Bake for 15 to 20 minutes or until bottom of bread is golden. Eat warm with cinnamon sugar, honey, or jam, or use cold for a unique sandwich.

45-Minute Breadsticks or No-Fail Deep-Dish Pizza Dough

Every time I make these breadsticks for company, they're a big hit. The pizza dough is great too; try it with half whole-wheat flour and half all-purpose flour.

2½ c. very warm water

5 t. instant yeast*

2 t. sugar

3 t. oil

1 t. salt

6 c. flour (half all-purpose and half
     whole-wheat, or all whole-wheat)

1 to 2 cubes of butter

Pour very warm water in mixing bowl. Sprinkle yeast on top and allow to dissolve. Add sugar, salt, and oil. Gradually add approximately 6

129

cups of flour. Turn oven to 400° F and melt 1 to 2 cubes of butter on cookie sheet as the oven preheats. Place dough on cookie sheet and press to fill pan, making sure butter gets on top of the dough. Allow to double in size (about 10 to 15 minutes). Cook for 10 to 12 minutes or until desired browning is accomplished. Cut into strips for breadsticks or top with favorite pizza toppings and place back in oven until cheese is melted (about 5 to 7 minutes). *Or 2 tablespoons regular yeast.

Cornbread

The best cornbread you've ever had!

½ c. butter

1 c. buttermilk (3 T. dry milk powder +
 1 c. water + 1 T. white vinegar or
 lemon juice; mix and let stand for
 5 minutes)

1 c. yellow cornmeal

1 c. flour (any combination of whole-
 wheat and all-purpose)

2/3 c. sugar

2 medium eggs (2 T. dry egg powder +
 ¼ c. water)

½ t. soda

½ t. salt

Preheat oven to 375° F. Melt butter; add to sugar and stir well. Add eggs and beat until well blended. Combine buttermilk and soda and stir into egg mixture. Add cornmeal, flour, and salt; stir until just blended. Pour into a greased 8-inch square pan. Bake at 375° F for about 30 minutes or until bread begins to pull away from sides of pan. Serve hot with butter and honey. Note: For glass pan, reduce oven temperature to 350° F. Recipe may be doubled; use 9x13-inch pan and increase baking time by 5 to 10 minutes.

Sandwich Pockets, page 128

STEP 7
USING DRIED BEANS

Reduced-Fat Devil's Food Bundt Cake, page 151

STEP 7

USING DRIED BEANS

The Wonderful, Versatile Bean

Now it's time to learn how to cook and use dried beans. With beans, you can make a hearty, filling, meatless meal for a fraction of the price of a meal that includes meat. And in case you didn't know, freshly cooked beans taste much better than canned beans. Beans are also extremely versatile. Not only can they be an important part of breakfast, lunch, or dinner, but they can also be substituted for fat in some of your favorite desserts! Imagine a protein- and fiber-filled dessert that is low in fat and that actually tastes just as good as the original.

You've Come So Far

Make sure you don't stop cooking with powdered milk, powdered eggs, and whole wheat. My recipes won't stop either; the amounts of fresh milk, fresh eggs, and all-purpose flour will be followed by the amounts of powdered milk, powdered eggs, and whole-wheat flour that may be substituted.

Beans: The Musical "Fruit"

We can't talk about cooking with and eating beans without discussing their one negative side effect. Our bodies lack the enzymes needed to digest some of the natural sugars contained in beans. When food can't be digested, it is left to ferment in the digestive track, creating gas. While intestinal gas is a natural part of life, the amount that can be caused by beans can be uncomfortable and embarrassing. Here are some ways to significantly decrease that gas:

1. Use enzyme tablets, such as Beano®, that help your body digest beans. For a free sample of Beano®, call the company's hotline at 1-800-257-8650.

2. Before cooking beans, soak them for at least three hours but preferably overnight. Change the soaking and cooking water at least two or three times.

3. Start eating beans more frequently. The more you eat beans, the more your body will become accustomed to them. Start out slowly with small amounts and gradually work up to larger amounts. The end goal is one cup of beans at least two to three times a week per person. (That will get you more nutrition, and you'll be rotating your food storage at the same time.)

Using Dehydrated Refried Beans

Of the beans offered at Church canneries, dehydrated refried beans are the easiest and quickest to cook. If you're unsure about using dehydrated refried beans, know this: they are the best-kept secret of most fast-food Mexican restaurants. That's right—there are dehydrated refried beans in that burrito! If restaurants can use dehydrated refried beans in their expensive food, why not use them in your own cooking—and save money while you're at it? The beans taste great and are easy to prepare, and your family will never guess that you are using dried refried beans.

Recipe for Cooking Dehydrated Refried Beans

Refried Beans

1 c. boiling water

1 c. dehydrated refried beans

Add dehydrated refried beans to boiling water and stir. Cover and let sit for 10 minutes.

Tips for Using Dehydrated Refried Beans in Your Recipes

1. Try them in burritos or tacos, where there are other flavors interacting with

the flavor of the refried beans.

2. Use the refried beans as a side dish with Mexican food. Be sure to serve them the same way you would from the can or from scratch, i.e., topping with sour cream, cheese, green onions, etc.

3. Get the consistency right. Decrease or increase the amount of water to make the beans just how your family likes them. My family likes the refried beans a little thicker, so I decrease the water, using ¾ cup water for each cup of dehydrated refried beans.

Action Steps

Try using dehydrated refried beans three times. You can try them as a side dish or in burritos, or try some of my favorite recipes. Commit to it by filling in the recipes and dates below.

The three recipes I'll make using dehydrated refried beans are:

1._____/Date:_____

2._____/Date:_____

3._____/Date:_____

Chicken Tortilla Soup, page 136

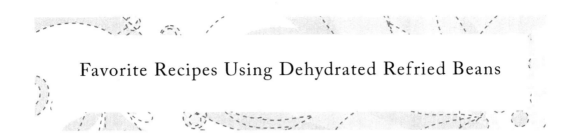

Favorite Recipes Using Dehydrated Refried Beans

7-Layer Bean Dip

This is my favorite appetizer to make for a big crowd. It is so easy and goes so fast.

1½ lb. ground beef

2 c. refried beans

4 c. shredded cheddar–Monterey Jack
    cheese blend

1 container (8 oz.) sour cream

1 c. guacamole

1 c. salsa

1 can (6 oz.) black olives, chopped

½ c. chopped tomatoes

½ c. chopped green onions

In a large skillet, brown ground beef. Set aside to drain and cool to room temperature.

Spread the beans into the bottom of a 9x13-inch serving tray that is at least 1½ inches deep. Sprinkle 2 cups of shredded cheese on top of beans. Sprinkle beef on top of cheese. Carefully spread sour cream on top of beef. Spread guacamole on top of sour cream. Pour salsa over guacamole and spread evenly. Sprinkle remaining shredded cheese on top of salsa. Sprinkle black olives, tomatoes, and green onions on top. Refrigerate overnight and serve cold.

Chicken Tortilla Soup

This soup is a great way to use leftover refried beans.

2 cans (14.5 oz.) diced tomatoes

1 can (4.5 oz.) diced green chiles

2 cans (14.5 oz.) chicken broth

1 can (14.5 oz.) whole kernel corn,
    drained

2 c. refried beans

2 c. shredded cooked chicken

corn chips

shredded Monterey Jack cheese

Combine tomatoes, green chiles, and broth in medium saucepan. Stir in beans and corn. Bring to a boil; reduce heat to low and simmer 5 minutes, stirring frequently. Add chicken; heat through. Top with corn chips and cheese.

Mike's Famous Bean Dip

My brother-in-law Mike makes this amazing dip when we watch football games at his house.

2 c. refried beans (made from

dehydrated refried beans, of course)

2 c. shredded cheddar cheese

1 pkg. (8 oz.) cream cheese

½ c. milk (1½ T. dry powdered milk +

½ c. water)

1 pkg. onion soup mix

¼ t. cayenne pepper

⅛ t. ground cumin seed

In a 2-quart saucepan over low heat, combine beans, cheeses, milk, soup mix, pepper, and cumin until well blended. Heat, stirring occasionally, until bubbly. Serve immediately with tortilla chips.

Mexican Lasagna

Delicious and easy!

1 lb. ground beef

1 jar (12 oz.) thick and chunky salsa

6 tostada shells or halved taco shells

1 c. refried beans

1 c. sour cream

4 oz. cheddar cheese, shredded (about

1 cup)

shredded lettuce for garnish

In skillet, brown beef; drain. Stir in ½ cup salsa. Spread ¼ cup salsa in 10-inch pie plate; top with 3 tostado shells or halved taco shells. Top with half of the refried beans, half of the meat mixture, and half of the sour cream and cheese. Repeat layers; cover with foil. Bake at 350° F for 30 minutes. Top with lettuce, remaining salsa, and sour cream. Makes 6 to 8 servings.

Refried Bean Burritos

These are great to serve for a crowd, and people love to pick their own toppings.

6 flour tortillas

2 c. refried beans

2 c. shredded cheddar cheese

salsa

137

Any or all of the following to taste:

    chopped tomato

    shredded lettuce

    sliced black olives

    sliced green onion

    sour cream

    guacamole or diced avocados

Place warm refried beans down center of tortilla and top with cheese. Warm in microwave until cheese is melted. Top with a combination of your favorite toppings and roll up like a burrito.

Double-Decker Mexican Pizzas

These tasty little pizzas will have you saying, "Ole!"

    1 lb. ground beef

    1 pkg. taco seasoning mix

    1 can (16 oz.) refried beans (1 c.
        dehydrated refried beans + 1 c.
        water; for thicker refried beans, use
        1¼ c. dehydrated refried beans)

    1¼ c. cheddar cheese, shredded

    1 large tomato, chopped

    ½ c. green onions, chopped

    ⅔ c. sour cream

    10 fajita-size (6-inch) flour tortillas

    salsa

Preheat oven to 400° F. Cook meat with taco seasoning mix as directed on package. Spread each of 5 tortillas with 2 tablespoons beans, ¼ cup seasoned meat, and 2 tablespoons cheese. Top each with second tortilla and additional layer of beans, meat, and cheese. Sprinkle with tomatoes and green onions. Place on baking sheet. Bake 8 to 10 minutes or until pizzas are heated through and cheese is melted. Top with salsa and sour cream.

Mexican Lasagna, page 137

Using Dried Whole Beans

Because most dried beans are prepared in essentially the same way, we will talk about white, pinto, and black beans in the same section. We'll review the characteristics of these common beans, then go over basic soaking and cooking instructions. Next, I'll share tips for incorporating beans into your own recipes.

Types of Beans

White Beans (Navy Beans)

Isn't it strange that a bean that is white in color is sometimes called a navy bean? Actually "navy" has nothing to do with the bean's color but rather refers to its use in a famous soup served in the Navy. The beans are small and are commonly used in soups, baked beans, chili, and ethnic dishes. Their flavor is light and almost buttery.

Pinto Beans

The pinto bean is actually a milder-tasting variety of the kidney bean, which was first cultivated by natives of South and Central America. The pinto bean is most commonly used in Mexican dishes such as refried beans, ranch-style beans, refritos charros, burritos, and tostadas. (See *Dry Beans and Peas,* Utah State Extension Service; http://extension.usu.edu/boxelder/files/uploads/fn207.pdf.)

Black Beans

Black beans are also known as turtle beans. These beans, which have a stronger flavor than pinto beans and white beans, are commonly paired with rice as a side dish and used in Oriental, Mediterranean, and Southern United States cooking.

Soaking Beans

Dried beans should be soaked before cooking to restore moisture, reduce cooking time, and, most importantly, to cut down on the gas they can produce inside of you. Choose a pot that will be large enough to give the beans room to expand as they soak. (Most beans, when hydrated, will triple in size.) There are two ways to soak beans—the quick method and the overnight method. The quick method takes about an hour and is a lifesaver if you didn't decide last night to make beans today. However, if you know a day in advance that you'll be making beans, use the overnight method, because it's easy, it works while you're sleeping, and the beans will be ready to cook in the morning. After the beans have soaked, discard any that have floated to the top because they may be hollow or ruined by mold or insects.

Quick Soaking

For each pound (2 cups) of dried beans, add 10 cups hot water; heat to boiling and let boil 2 to 3 minutes. Remove from heat, cover, and set aside for at least 1 hour.

Overnight Soak

For each pound (2 cups) of dried beans, add 10 cups cold water, then let soak overnight, or at least 8 hours.

Cooking Beans

Once your beans have soaked and tripled in size, it's time to cook them. Be sure to drain off the soaking water and rinse the beans, as the soaking water now contains some of the bean sugars that can cause gas. Depending on the variety, beans take 30 minutes to 2 hours to cook; check the package for more specific directions. Beans are done when they are tender but not falling apart. If the beans have been sitting in your food storage for a long time, you will need to cook them longer. When the beans are done, cool them in their cooking liquid if you are not adding them to another liquid, like a soup.

> *Tip: Because soaking and cooking dried beans takes time, you may want to cook more than you need and save them for next time. Store cooked beans tightly covered in the refrigerator up to five days, or in the freezer for up to six months.*

Tips for Using Beans in Your Recipes

1. Plan! Start early and make sure you have enough time to soak and cook your beans.

2. Don't forget the Beano®! Don't suffer through the aftermath of beans. Simply place the Beano® next to the salt and pass it around, or place one tablet on each person's dinner plate.

3. Look for use chili or soup recipes that call for canned beans, and use freshly cooked beans instead.

4. Cut the fat in baked goods while adding in protein and fiber! Substitute cooked and mashed beans for oil or butter in baked goods. These substitutions work especially well with cake and brownies. Baked goods that contain beans instead of butter or oil will have a lighter, fluffier texture. Remember, you can always start by using half mashed beans and half oil if you're worried your family won't like it.

Mashing Beans as a Substitute for Butter, Margarine, or Oil

Soak, cook, and drain beans as instructed previously, reserving the cooking water. Substitute beans for oil, margarine, or butter in baked goods, using the same amount of cooked beans as the type of fat called for. For recipes where butter or margarine is creamed with sugar, simply place whole, cooked beans with the sugar, then cream together. The dough may be moister than usual, so if you're also using powdered eggs, DO NOT add the water, since the liquid in the beans will rehydrate the eggs. (If the recipe is for cookies, be sure to grease the cookie sheet.) For recipes calling for oil, make a bean purée by placing cooked beans in a blender, then adding just enough water to blend beans into a smooth, thick paste with no chunks. Match the bean with the color of the treat you're making, so that the color of the treat doesn't change. For example, black beans work great in chocolate-based baked goods, and white beans work great in yellow cake.

Don't Just Take My Word for It

Here are some of the comments I've received about beans on my website.

"I made the low-fat chocolate bundt cake last night. I didn't tell my husband there were beans in it. He said he liked it and then I told him there were beans inside! Thanks for the great tip, and I was full after one piece." —Nichole

"I love putting beans in [my] cookies because beans are loaded with fiber and protein."—Brooke S.

"I did this the other day [substituted beans for oil] with the brownies, and my 8-year-old said they were the best brownies he had ever had!"— Shaylynn

Action Steps

Try using each type of bean three times in a different recipe. You can try them in soups, chilis, as a substitute for butter or oil in baking, or in some of my favorite recipes. Commit to it by filling in the recipes and dates below.

The three recipes I'll make with white beans are:

1._____/Date:_____

2._____/Date:_____

3._____/Date:_____

The three recipes I'll make with pinto beans are:

1._____/Date:_____

2._____/Date:_____

3._____/Date:_____

The three recipes I'll make with black beans are:

1._____/Date:_____

2._____/Date:_____

3._____/Date:_____

Favorite Recipes Using White Beans

Delicious Reduced-fat Oatmeal Raisin Cookies

With this cookie, you get the protein and fiber of beans, and you won't even miss the butter.

1 c. butter (1 c. whole cooked white beans)

1 c. brown sugar

1 c. white sugar

2 eggs (2 T. dry egg powder; omit water)

1 t. vanilla

1½ c. whole-wheat flour

1 t. salt

1 t. soda

3 c. quick-cooking oats

2 t. cinnamon

2 c. raisins, soaked in warm water for 15 minutes and drained

Cream together butter (or beans), sugars, eggs, and vanilla. Stir flour, salt, soda, oats, cinnamon, and raisins into creamed mixture. If dough is too dry using beans, slowly add in small amounts of water until dough is thick and slightly moist. Dough will be sticky. Drop by rounded tablespoonfuls onto greased cookie sheet. Bake at 375° F for 8 to 10 minutes.

Reduced-fat Yellow Birthday Cake

A great way to celebrate a birthday and sneak in some food storage!

1 pkg. (18.25 oz.) yellow cake mix

1 c. water

⅓ c. oil (⅓ c. white bean purée)

3 extra large eggs (⅓ c. dry powdered

eggs + ⅔ c. water)

frosting

Preheat oven to 350° F. Grease sides of baking pan. Blend ingredients in large bowl at low speed until moistened, about 3 seconds. Then beat at medium speed for 2 minutes. Pour batter in pans and bake immediately. Check cake-mix box for specific baking times. Cool cake completely, then frost.

White Bean and Sausage Rigatoni

This dish is fresh, simple, and filling—perfect for a cold evening.

8 oz. dried macaroni

2 c. cooked white beans

1 can (14.5 oz.) stewed tomatoes

2 t. Italian seasoning

6 oz. cooked Italian sausage, halved lengthwise and cut into ½-inch slices

⅓ cup fresh basil, snipped

1 oz. Asiago or Parmesan cheese, finely shredded (optional)

Cook pasta according to package directions. Drain. Return pasta to hot saucepan; cover to keep warm.

Meanwhile, in a large saucepan combine beans, undrained tomatoes, and sausage; heat through. Add pasta and basil; toss gently to combine. If desired, sprinkle individual servings with Asiago cheese.

Reduced-fat Chocolate-Chip Cookies

My mom used this recipe when I was growing up. It's just as delicious when I use beans instead of butter!

1 c. butter (1 c. white beans)

1 c. white sugar

1 c. brown sugar

2 eggs (2 T. dry powdered eggs; omit water)

1–2 t. vanilla

2 c. all-purpose flour (I use whole-wheat flour)

1½—3 c. old-fashioned oats, pulverized in blender

¾ t. salt

1 t. baking soda

1 t. baking powder

12 oz. chocolate chips

Cream together butter (beans) and sugars. Add eggs and vanilla. Mix flour, oatmeal, salt, baking soda, and baking powder into creamed mixture. If dough is too dry using beans, slowly add in small amounts of water until dough is thick and slightly moist. (Dough will be sticky.) Slowly stir in chocolate chips. Drop by rounded teaspoonfuls onto greased baking sheet. Bake at 375° F for 10 to 12 minutes. (Take cookies out of the oven before they look done or they will be too crispy.)

Southwestern White Chili

This chili is full of flavor and has a bit of a kick.

    1 c. chopped onion

    4 cloves garlic, minced

    2 t. ground cumin

    1 t. dried oregano, crushed

    ¼ t. ground red pepper

    2½ c. dried white beans, cooked and rinsed

    2 cans (4 oz.) diced green chiles

    1¼ c. chicken broth

    3 cans (10 oz.) chicken, undrained

    2 c. shredded Monterey Jack or pepper Jack cheese

    sour cream

In a 3½- to 6-quart slow cooker, place the onion, garlic, cumin, oregano, red pepper, beans, green chiles, broth, and cooked chicken. Stir to combine. Cover and cook on LOW setting for 7 to 8 hours or on HIGH setting for 3½ to 4 hours. Stir in the cheese until melted. Ladle the chili into 8 bowls. If desired, top with sour cream and sprinkle with additional green chiles or chives.

Baked Beans

Making baked beans from scratch can save you money . . . and they taste much better than the canned variety.

    1 lb. dry white beans, soaked and cooked

    2 c. reserved water from cooking beans

    1 quart water

    ½ t. salt

    1 medium onion, chopped

    2 T. prepared yellow mustard

    2 T. brown sugar

    2 T. molasses

    1 c. barbeque sauce

Combine beans, onion, mustard, brown sugar, molasses, barbeque sauce, bacon, and 1 cup cooking water in a 9x13-inch pan. Cover and bake at 400° F for 45 minutes or until mixture reaches the desired thickness, stirring occasionally. If mixture is too thick, add bean cooking water until desired consistency is reached.

Favorite Recipes Using Pinto Beans

Pinto Bean Fudge

Everyone will be shocked when you tell them this fudge is made with pinto beans, but don't tell them until they've tried it!

1 c. cooked pinto beans, drained and
　　mashed into a thick paste
¼ c. evaporated milk (1½ T. dry
　　powdered milk + ¼ c. water)
1 T. vanilla
6 oz. unsweetened chocolate
6 T. butter or margarine
2 lbs. powdered sugar
pecans or walnuts (optional)

In large bowl, stir beans and milk together, adding milk until the mixture resembles mashed potatoes; stir in vanilla. Melt chocolate and butter or margarine and stir into bean mixture.

Gradually stir in powdered sugar. Knead with hands until well blended. Spread into lightly greased 9-inch baking dish or form into two 1½-inch rolls. Chill 1 to 2 hours before serving.

Homemade Refried Beans

My good friend Mary brought this dish to a recipe swap and it was a big hit.

2 c. cooked pinto beans, drained (save
　　water from cooking)
1 c. cheddar cheese, grated
½ t. salt
¼ c. oil
½ t. garlic powder

Place drained cooked beans in a large frying pan on medium heat. Add the salt and garlic powder and mash the beans as they fry. When the beans begin to crisp, add a little water until they reach the desired consistency. Then add the cheese and turn off the heat. Stir the cheese into the beans and serve.

Reduced-fat Spice Cake with Pinto Beans

This is a great dessert to make during the holidays, when everything else is high in fat.

1 pkg. (18.25 oz.) spice cake mix

1⅓ c. water

⅓ c. oil (⅓ c. pinto bean purée)

3 extra large eggs (⅓ c. dry powdered

    eggs + ⅔ c. water)

frosting (vanilla or cream cheese)

Preheat oven to 350° F. Grease sides of baking pan. Blend ingredients in large bowl at low speed until moistened—about 3 seconds. Beat at medium speed for 2 minutes. Pour batter in pans and bake immediately. Check cake-mix box for specific baking times. Let cake cool completely before frosting.

Pinto Bean Pecan Pie

Trust me, this pie tastes much better than it sounds!

1 t. cornmeal

1 (9-inch) unbaked piecrust

2 eggs (3 T. dry egg powder + ⅔ c.

    water)

1½ c. white sugar

½ c. butter

1 t. vanilla extract

½ c. pinto beans, cooked and drained

½ c. pecan halves

Preheat oven to 350° F. Sprinkle 1 teaspoon of cornmeal in bottom of piecrust and set aside. Beat eggs in a large bowl (or if you're using powdered eggs, mix dry egg powder with water). Beat in sugar, butter, vanilla, and pinto beans. Pour filling into piecrust. Arrange pecans on top of pie. Bake for 60 minutes or until pie is golden brown and filling is set.

Mock Pumpkin Pie

This delicious pie packs a protein and fiber punch.

2 c. pinto bean purée

3 eggs (3 T. dry powdered eggs + ⅓ c.

    water)

1 can (13 oz.) evaporated milk (1½ T.

    dry powdered milk + ¼ c. water)

1 c. sugar

¾ t. salt

1 t. ground cinnamon

1 t. ground ginger

¼ t. ground cloves

¼ t. ground nutmeg

9-inch unbaked single piecrust

Purée 2 cups rinsed, unseasoned beans with ¼ to ½ cup water or chicken stock in a blender until smooth. Scrap down sides occasionally.

Add remaining ingredients (except piecrust) to blender in order given. Mix well, then pour into piecrust. Bake in a preheated 425° F oven for 15 minutes. Reduce temperature to 350° F and continue baking for 45 minutes or until knife inserted in center of pie filling comes out clean. Cool. Garnish with whipped cream, if desired.

Pioneer Soup

This hearty soup makes a great one-pot meal.

1¼ c. dry pinto beans

3 c. cold water

½ to 1 lb. ground beef

½ c. chopped onion

½ c. green pepper, finely diced

1 can (16 oz.) whole kernel corn,
　　undrained

1 can (16 oz.) diced tomatoes,
　　undrained

½ t. chili powder

¾ t. salt

½ c. shredded sharp cheddar cheese

In large saucepan, place washed and drained beans, and cold water. Bring to a boil. Cover and simmer 2 minutes. Remove from heat and let stand for 1 hour. Return to heat and simmer 1 hour and 15 minutes. In skillet, cook ground beef, chopped onion, and green pepper until meat is browned and vegetables are tender. Drain fat. Add meat mixture, corn, tomatoes, chili powder, and salt to taste. Simmer 20 minutes. Combine 1 tablespoon flour with 2 tablespoons water. Stir into stew. Cook and stir until thickened and bubbly. Stir in cheese.

Pioneer Soup

Favorite Recipes Using Black Beans

Black-Bean Nachos

Whether you serve these nachos as a snack or dinner, your family will love them!

Topping Suggestions:

> cheese
>
> cooked black beans, drained
>
> cooked ground beef
>
> corn
>
> olives
>
> tomatoes
>
> avocado or guacamole
>
> salsa
>
> sour cream
>
> yellow or green onions
>
> jalapenos or green chiles

Family Style

Turn on oven broiler. Cover a cookie sheet with tortilla chips. Top with cheese and cooked beans and/or meat. Place under broiler for about five minutes. Watch closely or the cheese will burn. Add other toppings when chips come out of oven, or let everyone put some chips on his or her plate and add toppings.

Individual Style

Place tortilla chips on each plate and top with cheese and cooked beans and/or meat. Heat in microwave until cheese is melted, then add desired toppings.

Ultimate Black-Bean Quesadillas

An easy and appetizing fiesta-style meal.

> 8 small tortillas (taco size)
>
> 2 c. cheese

149

1 c. diced chicken

1 c. canned corn, drained

1 c. cooked black beans, drained

1 can (4 oz.) diced green chiles
     (optional)

sour cream

salsa

guacamole

Heat skillet to medium heat. Place one tortilla on ungreased skillet, top with a portion of cheese, chicken, corn, black beans, and chiles. Top with another tortilla. Turn frequently until cheese is melted and quesadilla is warmed through. Remove from heat and cut into four triangles. Repeat with remaining tortillas and toppings. Serve with sour cream, salsa, and guacamole.

Reduced-Fat Peanut Butter Brownies

These delectable brownies taste just like the high-fat version.

1 pkg. (18.3 oz.) brownie mix

¼ c. water

½ c. oil (½ c. black bean purée)

2 eggs (2 T. dry powdered eggs + ¼ c. water)

1 c. peanut butter chips

Preheat oven to 350° F. Mix ingredients until just moistened. Pour into greased pan and bake immediately. Check brownie mix package for baking times for your pan and altitude. *Tip: Replacing all of the oil with black beans will create a cake-like brownie. If you like your brownies chewy, replace only half of the oil with puréed black beans.*

Devil's Food Cake-Mix Cookies

Try using chocolate, peanut butter, mint, white chocolate, or toffee chips to create a completely different cookie.

1 pkg. (18.25 oz.) devil's food cake mix
     (not a regular chocolate cake mix)

½ c. butter, softened (½ c. whole black beans, cooked)

1 t. vanilla

2 eggs (2 T. dry powdered eggs; omit water)

½ c. chopped nuts

1 c. semisweet chocolate chips (or chips of your choice)

Preheat oven to 350° F. Place butter, vanilla, eggs, and half of the dry cake mix in a large bowl. Mix with hand mixer on medium speed until smooth. If dough is too dry using beans, slowly add in small amounts of water until dough is thick and slightly moist. Stir in nuts, chocolate chips, and remaining cake mix. Dough will be sticky. Drop dough by rounded tablespoonfuls (about 2 inches apart) onto ungreased cookie sheet. Bake for 10 to 12 minutes.

Reduced-Fat Devil's Food Bundt® Cake

A great treat when you want to eat healthier!

1 pkg. (18.25 oz.) devil's food cake mix

1⅓ c. water

½ c. oil (½ c. black bean purée)

3 extra large eggs (⅓ c. dry powdered

    eggs + ⅔ c. water)

Preheat oven to 350° F. Grease sides of Bundt® pan. Blend ingredients in large bowl at low speed until moistened, about 3 seconds. Beat at medium speed for 2 minutes. Pour batter in pan and bake immediately. Check cake-mix box for specific baking times. Allow cake to cool in pan for 5 minutes before turning out onto cooling rack. Dust with powdered sugar when completely cool.

Black Beans and Corn

A very tasty alternative to plain black beans.

2 c. cooked blacked beans, drained

1 c. reserved cooking water from beans

1 can whole kernel corn, drained

1 c. onion, chopped

½ c. bell pepper, chopped

1 t. cumin

1–2 T. garlic salt

1 T. lemon juice

Combine ingredients in 2-quart saucepan and simmer over low heat for 10 minutes.

Black-Bean Salsa

If you love beans, this salsa will be your new favorite.

2 c. cooked black beans, drained

½ c. sliced green onions

1 c. chopped tomatoes

2 c. canned corn, drained

½–1 t. ground cumin

½ t. chopped jalapeno peppers

salt (to taste)

Combine ingredients in a small bowl. Serve with tortilla chips.

Southwestern Ranch Salad

This salad is perfect on a hot summer day.

6 c. romaine lettuce, chopped

2 c. barbeque chicken, cubed

1 c. cooked black beans

1 c. canned corn

2 tomato, chopped

1 cucumber, sliced and quartered

1 avocado, chopped

½ c. Monterey Jack cheese

ranch dressing

Combine and toss ingredients.

Citrus Black-Bean Salad

This unique dish will make your taste buds tingle.

4 c. cooked black beans

2 large oranges, peeled, sectioned

2/3 c. thinly sliced green onions

1/3 c. salsa

¼ c. lime juice

2 cloves garlic, minced

½ t. ground cumin

lettuce leaves

tortilla chips

Mix all ingredients except lettuce and crackers in bowl, stirring gently. Refrigerate at least 2 hours to blend flavors. Serve salad on lettuce with chips.

Cowboy Soup

A great soup to warm you up.

2 c. cooked black beans

1 can (14½ oz.) diced tomatoes, undrained

1 can (4 oz.) diced green chiles, undrained

¾ lb. ground beef, cooked

3 cups water

1 c. frozen corn

1 small onion, chopped

3 cloves garlic, minced

1 T. ground cumin

½ t. hot pepper sauce

Mix all ingredients in large saucepan or Dutch oven. Bring to boil on medium-high heat; cover. Simmer on low heat 15 minutes, stirring occasionally. Serve with cheese and sour cream.

STEP 8

USING DRIED VEGETABLES AND FRUITS

Whole-Wheat Carrot Cake Muffins, page 172

STEP 8

USING DRIED VEGETABLES AND FRUITS

No More Peeling and Chopping

You're on the last step! You're cooking with powdered milk, powdered eggs, whole wheat, and beans in your own recipes on a consistent basis. Now it's time to learn more about dehydrated fruits and vegetables—and to start cooking with them.

Dehydrated fruits and vegetables can be substituted for fresh fruits and vegetables in many recipes. The best thing is, they've already been peeled and chopped, so you can skip those two messy, time-consuming tasks.

Make sure you don't stop cooking with powdered milk, powdered eggs, whole wheat, and beans. The recipes in this step will, of course, show these substitutions.

Potato Flakes

Using potato flakes instead of making mashed potatoes from fresh potatoes will save you time in both cooking and cleanup. In addition to making a great side dish, mashed potatoes made from potato flakes can be used in casseroles that call for mashed potatoes. And, as you learned in Step 7, adding potato flakes to bread and rolls will make them soft and chewy.

If your family prefers the taste of mashed potatoes from scratch, don't worry. I've got some tips to make those reconstituted potato flakes taste more like homemade mashed potatoes!

Making Basic Mashed Potatoes

To make mashed potatoes using dehydrated potato flakes, just add the potato flakes to an equal amount of boiling water and stir.

I also like to add milk, butter or margarine, and salt.

Mashed Potatoes

> 3 c. boiling water
>
> 3 c. potato flakes
>
> 1 t. salt
>
> ¼ c. butter or margarine
>
> 1 c. milk

Combine boiling water, salt, butter or margarine, and milk in a 2-quart saucepan. Add potato flakes and stir by hand until potatoes are dissolved. Makes 9 servings.

Tips for Using Potato Flakes to Make "Homemade" Mashed Potatoes

1. If you use my basic recipe, try substituting sour cream or cream cheese for part of the milk. This enhances the flavor of the potatoes and makes them smooth and creamy.

2. Use the same amount of butter, salt, and pepper you use when you make real homemade mashed potatoes.

3. Beat the potato flakes and water the same way you would beat homemade mashed potatoes. This adds air to the potatoes, making them fluffy—and it gives your family the illusion that you're making homemade mashed potatoes! (Be sure not to over-mix the potatoes.)

Action Steps

Try using potato flakes three times. You can try them as a side dish, in a casserole, or in some of my favorite recipes. Commit to it today by filling in the recipes and dates below.

The three recipes I'll make using potato flakes are:

1._____/Date:_____

2._____/Date:_____

3._____/Date:_____

Roasted Garlic Mashed Potatoes, page 160
Grilled Pork Chops with Apple-Cranberry Sauce, page 162

Favorite Recipes Using Potato Flakes

Deep-Dish Hamburger Pie

A scrumptious way to use those leftover mashed potatoes.

½ lb. ground beef

¼ c. chopped onion

¼ t. salt

⅛ t. pepper

1 c. mashed potatoes

3 T. shredded cheese

1 can (8 oz.) cut green beans, drained

½ can (10¾ oz.) tomato soup

½ c. ketchup

Heat oven to 350° F. In 8-inch skillet, cook meat and onion until meat is brown and onion is tender. Stir in seasonings, beans, and soup. Pour into ungreased 1-quart casserole dish. Spoon mashed potatoes on mixture and top with cheese. Bake until mixture is hot and top is slightly brown, about 30 minutes. Makes 4 to 6 servings.

Oven "Fried" Chicken

Everyone loves this chicken, and it's much less messy to make than the fried version.

3–4 lbs. chicken pieces

1 extra large egg (2 T. dry egg powder + ¼ c. water) and 2 T. milk (⅓ T. dry powdered milk + 2 T. water), beaten together

potato flakes for coating

¼ c. (½ stick) butter

Dip chicken pieces in egg–milk mixture, then dredge chicken parts in potato flakes to coat. Spread 2 tablespoons butter on a 10x15-inch baking pan with edges at least 1 inch high. Place chicken pieces skin side down on the buttered pan. Drizzle chicken pieces with melted butter. Bake in a preheated oven at 425° F for 25 minutes. Turn and bake about 20 to 25 minutes longer or until cooked through. Sprinkle with salt and pepper before removing from the pan. Best served hot. Makes 4 to 6 servings.

Thanksgiving Shepherd's Pie

Enjoy the taste of Thanksgiving anytime!

> 1½ c. cubed turkey, cooked
>
> 2 c. hot mashed potatoes
>
> ½ c. sour cream
>
> 1 c. shredded cheddar cheese, divided
>
> 1 bag frozen mixed vegetables, thawed
>
> 1 c. turkey gravy
>
> 1 pkg. (6 oz.) instant stuffing mix for turkey
>
> 1 can (16 oz.) whole cranberry sauce

Heat oven to 350° F. Prepare stuffing according to package directions, then stir in cranberry sauce and set aside. Mix potatoes, sour cream, and ½ cup shredded cheese; set aside. Stir vegetables and gravy into meat and spoon into 9-inch square baking dish. Cover with stuffing mix, then spread mashed potatoes on top. (Don't worry about making it perfectly even.) Sprinkle with remaining ½ cup shredded cheese. Bake for 20 minutes or until heated through. Makes 4 to 6 servings.

Mashed Potato Patties

A great side dish that your family will love.

> 2 c. mashed potatoes
>
> 1 extra large egg (2 T. dry powdered eggs + ¼ c. water)
>
> 2 T. milk
>
> 1 c. shredded cheddar cheese
>
> ¼ c. chopped onion, optional
>
> ½ c. chopped green pepper, optional
>
> 2½ c. crushed crackers or cornflake crumbs

Mix ingredients together. Form into patties. Roll each patty in crushed crackers or cornflake crumbs. Put on cookie sheet and bake in 350° F oven until hot. Remove from oven and move oven rack to highest position, then turn on oven broiler. Place cookie sheet back in oven for two minutes or until potato patties are brown on top (watch carefully so they don't burn). Serve hot. Makes 4 to 6 servings.

Roasted Garlic Mashed Potatoes

A great way to dress up mashed potatoes made from potato flakes. The garlic and rosemary compliment each other perfectly.

> 4 cloves garlic, peeled
>
> 2 T. fresh rosemary sprigs or 2 t. dried
>   rosemary
>
> 4 c. prepared mashed potatoes
>   (substitute sour cream for milk)

Roast garlic under oven broiler until brown, flipping once. (Watch carefully, as it cooks quickly.) Chop roasted garlic and add, along with rosemary, to prepared mashed potatoes. Makes 4 to 6 servings.

Instant Mashed-Potato Dumplings

A great addition to any broth-based soup.

> 1 c. potato flakes
>
> 1 c. flour
>
> 2 t. baking powder
>
> ½ t. salt
>
> 1 t. minced parsley
>
> 1 t. onion powder
>
> 1 c. milk (3 T. dry milk powder + 1 c.
>   water)

> 1 extra large egg (2 T. dry egg powder +
>   ¼ c. water)

Combine potato flakes, flour, baking powder, salt, and parsley. In a separate bowl, combine milk and egg. (If using powdered eggs and milk, combine dry ingredients before adding water). Add to dry ingredients and stir to moisten. Let stand 3 minutes. Drop by spoonful onto simmering liquid. Cover tightly and cook 10 to 15 minutes.

Thanksgiving Shepherd's Pie, page 159

Dried Apple Slices

With dried apples slices, you can create delicious desserts in a fraction of the time it would take using fresh apples. And in a pinch, you can use dried apple slices to make applesauce. Dried apple slices also taste great straight out of the can. So sample a few, and let's get baking.

Recipe for Rehydrating Dried Apple Slices

Combine equal parts apples and boiling water (for example, 1 cup dried apples and 1 cup boiling water). Let stand for at least 5 minutes.

Tips for Using Dried Apple Slices in Your Favorite Recipes

1. Eat them dry as a healthy alternative to potato chips. They are quite tasty!

2. Make your own applesauce. After hydrating apple slices, put them in blender and pulse until applesauce reaches the desired consistency. Then season to taste with sugar and cinnamon, or use in baking as a substitute for oil.

3. Skip a step. Use rehydrated dried apples in your favorite apple pie or cobbler and eliminate the hassle of washing, coring, peeling, and slicing the apples.

Action Steps

Try using dried apple slices three times. You can feed them to your family straight out of the can, use them in your favorite apple pie, or try some of my favorite recipes. Commit to it by filling in the recipes and dates below.

The three recipes I'll make using dried apple slices are:

1._____/Date:_____

2._____/Date:_____

3._____/Date:_____

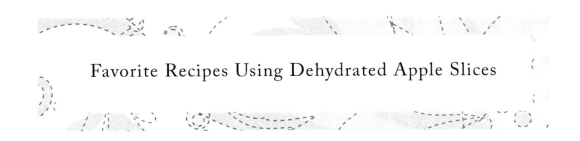

Favorite Recipes Using Dehydrated Apple Slices

Apple Brown Betty

This dessert is simple and delicious.

Filling

    2 c. boiling water

    4 c. dried apples silces

Topping

    ½ c. whole-wheat flour

    ¼ c. oatmeal

    ½ t. cinnamon

    ¼ c. brown sugar

    ¼ c. butter

Pour boiling water over dried apples. Let stand at least 5 minutes. Meanwhile, mix dry topping ingredients together, then cut in butter. Place apples and any remaining liquid in a greased 9-inch square baking pan. Sprinkle topping over apples. Bake at 350° F for 55 minutes.

Grilled Pork Chops with Apple-Cranberry Sauce

This dish is great for special occasions; it tastes like it's from a fancy restaurant.

    4 pork chops

    2 c. applesauce (2 c. dried apple slices

        + 2 c. boiling water; let stand for 5

        minutes and mix in blender)

    1 can (16 oz.) whole cranberry sauce

Combine applesauce and whole cranberry sauce and chill. Grill pork chops on hot grill for 15 to 20 minutes, turning one time until center is no longer pink. Top pork chops with apple-cranberry sauce and serve immediately.

German Apple Cake

This moist, flavorful cake will make everyone think you spent hours in the kitchen.

2 extra large eggs (¼ c. dry powdered
   eggs + ½ c. water)

1 c. oil (1 c. white bean purée)

1 t. vanilla

4 c. peeled and thinly sliced apples (3 c.
   dried apple slices + 6 c. boiling
   water; let stand for five minutes and
   drain excess water)

2 c. flour (I use half whole-wheat and
   half all-purpose)

2 t. cinnamon

½ t. salt

2 c. sugar

1 t. baking soda

1 c. pecans or walnuts, chopped
(optional)

whipped cream or whipped topping

Beat 2 large eggs until foamy. Add oil (or bean purée) and vanilla. Mix dry ingredients together and add to wet mixture. Batter will be very thick. With a sturdy spoon or clean hands, mix in 4 cups peeled and thinly sliced apples. Pour batter into a greased and floured 9x13-inch baking pan.

Scatter nuts on top of cake before baking. Bake at 350° F for 45 to 60 minutes. Cool and serve with whipped cream.

Reduced-fat Banana Bread

This amazing bread won't last long once your family tastes it.

4 T. butter, softened

¼ c. applesauce (¼ c. dried apple slices
   + ¼ c. boiling water; let stand for
   five minutes and mix in blender)

2 eggs (2 T. dry powdered eggs + ¼ c.
   water)

2 T. skim milk or water

¾ c. brown sugar

1 c. mashed banana (2 to 3 medium
   bananas)

1¾ c. whole-wheat flour

2 t. baking powder

½ t. baking soda

¼ t. salt (optional)

¼ c. walnuts or pecans, coarsely
chopped (optional)

Beat butter, applesauce, eggs, milk, and brown sugar in large mixer bowl until smooth. Add banana and blend at low speed; beat at high speed 1 to 2 minutes. Combine flour, baking powder, baking soda, and salt; mix into batter. Mix in nuts. Pour batter into greased loaf pan. Bake at 350° F until bread is golden and toothpick inserted in center comes out clean (55 to 60 minutes). Cool in pan on wire rack for 10 minutes; remove from pan and cool to room temperature. *Tip: If you don't have two bread pans but want to double the recipe, you can bake the bread in a Bundt® pan. This works great for brunches or anytime you want to "dress up" the bread. Be sure to lengthen the baking time by 5 to 10 minutes when using a Bundt® pan.*

Dutch Apple Pie

This is my all-time-favorite apple pie, and it's so easy to make with dried apples.

Filling

> 2 c. dehydrated apples, firmly packed
>
> 2 c. boiling water
>
> ⅓ c. sugar
>
> 2 T. all-purpose flour
>
> ½ t. cinnamon

Topping

> ⅓ c. brown sugar
>
> ½ c. whole-wheat flour
>
> ¼ c. butter

Crust

> 1 single piecrust

Pour boiling water over apples and let sit for at least 5 minutes. Mix dry filling ingredients together and add to apple mix. Continue cooking until thick, stirring constantly to prevent scorching. Pour mixture into piecrust and dot with 1 tablespoon butter.

Mix together brown sugar and flour, then cut in butter until crumbly. Sprinkle topping over apple mixture and place pie in a 350° F oven for 55 minutes.

German Apple Cake, page 163

Dried Onion Flakes

Using dried onion flakes instead of fresh onions will save you money. And with no more chopping and no more cleanup, you'll save time, too. Best of all, there will be no more crying in the kitchen!

Recipe for Rehydrating Dried Onion Flakes

Combine one part onion flakes and two parts boiling water (for example, ¼ cup onion flakes and ½ cup boiling water). Let stand for five minutes or until hydrated (flakes should double in size). Drain off excess water before adding to a recipe. The equivalent of one small onion, chopped, is ¼ cup onion flakes.

Tips for Using Dried Onion Flakes in Your Favorite Recipes

1. No more tears! Use dried onion flakes in any recipe calling for chopped onions (except salads) and avoid the hassle of cutting them yourself.

2. Skip a step! If you're adding dried onions to a sauce or soup, you don't need to hydrate them first. Simply add the onions while the sauce or soup simmers; the liquid will hydrate the onions.

3. Extra flavor. Add hydrated onion flakes to ground meat for extra flavor.

Action Steps

Try using dried onion flakes three times. You can add them to spaghetti sauce, chili, or ground beef, or you can try some of my favorite recipes. Commit to it by filling in the recipes and dates below.

The three recipes I'll make using dried onion flakes are:

1._____/Date:_____

2._____/Date:_____

3._____/Date:_____

Favorite Recipes Using Dried Onion Flakes

Homemade Onion Soup Mix

Use this in any recipe calling for onion soup mix; it will save you money!

4 t. beef bouillon granules

8 t. dried onion flakes

1 t. onion powder

¼ t. garlic salt

¼ t. ground pepper

Add ingredients to recipe in place of onion soup mix, or combine and store in baggies for future use.

Grilled Sautéed Onions

These taste great on steaks and burgers in the summertime.

1. Rehydrate onion flakes in water (use 2 parts water and 1 part onion). Remember that ¼ cup dried onions will equal one cup chopped onion once hydrated.

2. After letting onions sit in water for about 10 minutes, drain off excess water.

3. Wrap in aluminum foil with a little butter and grill for 5 to 7 minutes, turning once.

4. Voilà!—sautéed onions with no mess, no chopping, and in no time, thanks to food storage.

Cheeseburger Mac 'n' Cheese

Tastes just like a cheeseburger from a fast-food restaurant.

2 c. white sauce from Magic Mix (1⅓ c. Magic Mix + 2 c. water; mix together and stir constantly over medium heat until thickened)

2 c. uncooked macaroni

2 c. cheese

1–2 t. salt or garlic salt (optional)

½ c. ketchup

1 T. yellow mustard

1 lb. ground beef

¼ c. dried onion flakes hydrated
  in ½ c. warm water, drained
  (optional)

1 bag frozen mixed vegetables

Cook macaroni in boiling water until tender. Meanwhile, cook hamburger in frying pan until the meat is no longer pink. Drain macaroni. In the empty pot, make white sauce from Magic Mix. Combine all ingredients and heat through. Makes 4 servings.

Sloppy Joes

With this recipe, you save time and money by extending your ground beef with cracked wheat and by using dried onions.

1 lb. ground beef

1 medium onion, chopped (¼ c.
  dried onion flakes)

1 c. cracked wheat, cooked

1 can tomato soup

½ c. ketchup

2 t. brown sugar

1½ t. chili powder

1½ T. Worcestershire sauce

1 t. salt

1½ t. dry ground mustard

½ t. curry powder

8 hamburger buns

Cook beef in saucepan, stirring often. Drain meat. Add all recipe ingredients and simmer for 20 to 30 minutes. Serves 8.

Potato-Round Casserole

This recipe even sneaks in a green vegetable!

1 lb. hamburger, uncooked

¼ c. dried onion flakes

1 can (12.5 oz.) cream of mushroom
  soup (or cream of mushroom soup
  made from Magic Mix)

1 can (16.5 oz.) green beans, drained

1 small pkg. potato rounds (I use Tater
  Tots™)

Spread hamburger in a 9x13-inch pan. Sprinkle hamburger with salt, pepper, and onion. Pour and spread the mushroom soup on top of the hamburger. Drain the green beans, then spread over the soup.

Cover with potato rounds. Bake 1 hour at 350° F. Makes 6 servings.

Spaghetti Zucchini Bake

Other than the three fresh items, you probably have all these ingredients in your three-month or one-year supply!

1 lb. penne or macaroni pasta

1½ lb. Italian sausage, cooked and cut into bite-size pieces

2 cans (14 oz. each) diced tomatoes

1–2 cans (4.5 oz. each) mushrooms (optional)

1 can (3.9 oz.) tomato paste

¼ c. dried onion flakes

1–2 garlic cloves

4–5 c. zucchini, cut into large chunks

1 t. oregano

2 t. basil

2 c. mozzarella cheese, grated

salt to taste

Cook pasta in boiling water until tender. Combine diced tomatoes, mushrooms, tomato paste, dried onions, garlic, oregano, and basil in large pot. Heat to boiling and simmer for 5 to 10 minutes. While pasta cooks, grill sausage. Add zucchini and meat to sauce and simmer for 7 minutes. Add pasta and 1 cup cheese; stir. Place mixture in a 9x13-inch casserole dish and top with remaining cheese. Place under broiler until cheese is melted. Makes 6 servings. *Tip: Make this meal in the morning (do everything but broil it) and place in the refrigerator. To reheat, place in the oven at 350° F for 30 minutes or until the cheese is melted.*

Spaghetti Zucchini Bake

Dried Carrots

Dried carrots are extremely versatile and easy to use. Best of all, you don't have to grate, slice, or chop them! They can be used to make delicious carrot cakes, muffins, and cookies, or added to soups, sauces, and meat loaf to provide extra nutrition.

Recipe for Rehydrating Dried Carrots

Combine one part carrots and two parts cool water (for example, 1 cup carrots to 2 cups cool water). Let stand for 20 minutes then, drain. (If in a hurry, use warm water and let stand for 10 minutes.)

Tips for Using Dried Carrots in Your Favorite Recipes

1. Make meals more nutritious and flavorful. Add dried carrots to any soup with vegetables, to any tomato-based sauce, or to meat loaf.

2. Skip a step. If you're adding dried carrots to a sauce or soup, there is no need to hydrate them first. Simply add the carrots while your sauce simmers and they will hydrate while you're doing something else.

3. Make them smaller. Baked goods taste better with smaller pieces of dried carrots. Simply pulse the dried carrot pieces in your blender until they are about half their original size.

Action Steps

Try using dried carrots three times. You can add them to your spaghetti sauce, meat loaf, or carrot cake, or you can try some of my favorite recipes. Commit to it today by filling in the recipes and dates below.

The three recipes I'll make with dried carrots are:

1._____/Date:_____

2._____/Date:_____

3._____/Date:_____

Favorite Recipes Using Dried Carrots

Carrot Cake

This cake is so yummy that no one will guess it's made with only items from your food storage!

2 c. sugar

1½ c. vegetable oil

4 eggs (½ c. dry powdered eggs + 1 c.
  water) beaten

2 c. flour (I use half whole-wheat flour
  and half all-purpose flour)

2 t. baking soda

¼ t. salt

2 t. cinnamon

2–4 cups finely grated carrots (if using
  dried carrots, pulse them a few
  times in blender before hydrating
  them)

¾ c. nuts, coarsely chopped (optional)

In large bowl, mix together sugar, oil, and beaten eggs. In separate bowl, combine flour, soda, salt, and cinnamon. Stir dry mixture into wet mixture, then fold in carrots and nuts. Bake at 350° F for 40 to 50 minutes, or until the cake starts to pull away from the sides of the pan. Cool completely and frost with Best-Ever Cream Cheese Frosting (see page 127).

Spaghetti Sauce

This sauce tastes so much better than the kind you buy in the store.

2 T. olive or vegetable oil

1 c. fresh onion, chopped (¼ c.
  dried onion flakes)

2 small green bell pepper, chopped

1 c. fresh carrots, chopped (½ c.

dried carrots)

1 can (4.5 oz.) mushrooms, drained

2 large cloves garlic, minced or finely
chopped

2 cans (14½ oz.) diced tomatoes,
undrained

3–4 cans (8 oz.) tomato sauce

2 T. chopped fresh or 2 t. dried basil
leaves

1 T. chopped fresh or 1 t. dried oregano
leaves

½ t. salt

¼ t. pepper

Stovetop Directions

Heat oil in 3-quart saucepan over medium heat. Cook onion, bell pepper, and garlic in oil for 2 minutes, stirring occasionally. Stir in remaining ingredients. Heat to boiling; reduce heat. Cover and simmer 45 minutes. Use sauce immediately, or cover and refrigerate up to 2 weeks or freeze up to 1 year.

Slow Cooker Directions

Omit the oil. Mix the remaining ingredients together in 3½- to 6-quart slow cooker. Cover and cook on low for 6 to 8 hours.

Mom's Meat Loaf

If you use extra-leaf ground beef, this meat loaf is actually good for you!

1½ lb. ground beef, uncooked

¾ c. oatmeal

1 or 2 eggs (2 T. dry powdered eggs + ¼
c. water)

1 pkg. onion soup mix (4 t. beef
bouillon granules, 8 t. dried onion
flakes, 1 t. onion powder, ¼ t. garlic
salt, ¼ t. ground pepper)

¼ c. dry powdered milk

1 can (8 oz.) tomato sauce

½ c. dried carrots

Place dehydrated carrots in 1 cup warm water and let stand for 10 minutes. Mix ingredients together and place in greased loaf pan. Bake at 350° F for 1 hour.

Black-Bean Soup

A perfect way to combine ingredients from your pantry with ingredients from your one-year supply.

1½ c. fresh onion, chopped (or ⅓ c.
dried onion flakes)

1 T. olive oil

1 c. red bell pepper, chopped

4 cloves garlic, minced

1 can (14.5 oz.) diced tomatoes, undrained

1 can (4 oz.) diced green chiles

¾ c. dried carrots

1½ t. ground cumin

3 c. chicken broth

6 c. cooked black beans, drained (or four 15-oz. cans)

¼ c. red wine vinegar

Heat oil in large, deep saucepan. Sauté onion (if using fresh), bell pepper, and garlic until tender. Add remaining ingredients (including dried onions) and simmer for 10 minutes. Serve garnished with sour cream.

Whole-Wheat Carrot Cake Muffins

These muffins are delicious, easy to make, and—with pineapple, raisins, carrots, and whole wheat—quite nutritious.

2 c. brown sugar

1 c. oil (1 c. cooked white beans)

3 eggs (3 T. dry powdered eggs + ⅓ c. water)

2 c. carrots, finely grated (pulse 1 cup dried carrots in blender, then add 2 cups cold water and let sit for 20 minutes)

1 c. crushed pineapple, drained

3 c. whole-wheat flour

1 t. salt

1 T. baking soda

1 t. cinnamon

2 t. vanilla

1 c. raisins (soak in warm water for 10 minutes, then drain before adding to batter)

1 c. walnuts, coarsely chopped

Grease and flour two bread pans, one Bundt® pan, or two 12-cup muffin pans, or spray with cooking spray. Beat together brown sugar, oil, and eggs (no need to reconstitute eggs first; just add the required water to the mixture when you add egg powder). Stir in carrots and pineapple. Blend dry ingredients first, then combine thoroughly with batter. Add vanilla, raisins, and nuts. Pour into prepared pans and bake at 350° F. Bake loaves for 40 to 45 minutes, muffins for 20 minutes, and Bundt® for 1 hour, or until done.

Split-Pea Soup

A delicious way to eat your vegetables.

1 pkg. (16 oz.) dry split peas

1 ham bone

7 c. water

1 medium onion, chopped (¼ c. dried
   onion flakes)

2 medium carrots, chopped (½ c.
   dried carrots)

1 c. chopped celery

¾ t. salt

½ t. thyme

1 bay leaf

1 garlic clove, minced

Rinse peas under cold water in colander, removing any debris or blemished peas. Place peas, ham bone, and water in soup pot.

Add onion, carrots, salt, thyme, bay leaf, and pepper. Reduce heat and simmer, uncovered, for 1 hour and 15 minutes or until peas are tender, stirring constantly. Stir frequently near end of cooking to keep soup from scorching. Remove ham bone from pot, then take off as much meat as possible. Add meat to soup. Discard bone. Remove bay leaf and discard. Serve warm with biscuits.

Pressure Cooker Instructions

Place all ingredients in pressure cooker, with ham bone and vegetables on the bottom. Bring to pressure. Turn down pressure cooker until ticker is barely moving. Cook 20 minutes and run pressure cooker under cold water to stop the action before removing lid. Remove ham bone and take off as much meat as possible and add to soup. Discard bone. Remove bay leaf and discard. Serve warm with biscuits.

Black-Bean Soup, page 171

A Final Word

Helping Others

Now you're ready for the greatest aspect of food storage—the ability to have a little extra food on hand to share with others. Jesus taught, "Verily I say unto you, Inasmuch as ye have done it unto one of the least of these my brethren, ye have done it unto me" (Matt. 25:40). As you look at your food storage and think about all your blessings, I hope you'll be inspired to give—and give generously. Because you have food storage, you can now be an instrument in the hands of the Lord to help others in need. Look for opportunities to take people meals or to donate to food banks, or other ways you can use your food to help others.

Another way to help is to share with others what you have learned in this book—particularly if they think food storage isn't for them. Lend them this book or suggest that they check it out from the library. Pass along some of the e-mail links to my videos or handouts about food storage. Together, we can really change how people look at food storage.

You Can Do It

Keep it up! Keep giving your family the extra nutrition they need. And keep feeling the peace of knowing that if an emergency happens (an everyday one or a life crisis), you can feed your family with food they already enjoy.

Index